The Art of

Dreamcatching

How To Turn
ANY Dream Into A Reality

John Bourgeois

The Art of Dreamcatching
Copyright © 2020 by John Bourgeois

ISBN 978-0-578-99286-0

Dedication

I want to dedicate this book to all the Dreamcatchers that took the time to sow into my life and plant the seed of what it looks like to turn a dream into a reality.

I want to dedicate this book to all the Dreamcatchers, who don't know it yet, but they, themselves, are Dreamcatchers, and are on the cusp of achieving their own dream.

Table of Contents

Acknowledgements

I want to thank you, Dad and Mom, for being your own version of a Dreamcatcher while I was growing up. I want to take a moment to thank you, Kat and Terryl, for being Dreamcatchers in your industries and in your own genres. I want to thank you, Tiff, for telling me to pick the pen back up and continue to write even with life's hurdles.

I cannot forget you baby, my Angelique, and I want to thank you for allowing me to run after my dreams, for believing in me, for running alongside me, for picking me up in the moments where I scrape my knee, for hugging me, and being a comfort for me in those moments that I cried.

Ezekiel, Jaxon, Annabelle, Mikayla, Vaeh, and Atlas, you don't know this, but you come from a long line of Dreamcatchers. Don't allow any obstacle, any hurdle, or anything else to tell you differently. Go and make your dreams a reality. I love you

Introduction: "Hi, My Name is John" (sung to the sound of Eminem's - "My Name Is")

Let's get formalities out of the way:

Who am I? Or better yet, who is John Bourgeois?

Well, you probably know me from my first book, The Pen and Its Author, saw that I had written another book, and thought to yourself, "The Pen and Its Author was an amazing book. I have to get my hands on another one of John's remarkable works."

No? Okay, then you must know me from the top-rated Apple podcast, The Dreamcatchers Show, where I interviewed top-rated, world-class, Dreamcatchers and we'll talk later on this, so do not worry. For now, when you see 'Dreamcatcher,' just think 'Badass, go-getters,' who are doing extraordinary things across the globe.

No? Then maybe, just maybe, you picked up this book because you are like me a decade ago. You are browsing online or searching the bookstores' bookshelves for anything or everything that could help you figure out how to take the idea that is in your head and in your heart and turn it into reality. You saw the title of the book, thought, 'I have no clue what Dreamcatching is,' but saw the phrase "how to turn ANY dream into reality," and decided to give this book a try.

Hoping, just hoping, that maybe this was the holy grail of books that will finally help you achieve your dreams. Well, the truth is...

It is!!
The author, himself, told me.

All kidding aside, fifteen years ago, I was in the exact same space you are. I had this dream. I didn't know what to do with it. I had tried several times to give it life with failed attempts. I was lost. I was depressed. I was down and out. I was wishing that someone would come along and just give me a hand, show me what I was missing, and help me along the way to my dreams.

My desire is that this is the last book you ever need to read before you start turning your dreams into reality.
It is my futile attempt at going back in time, finding Sarah Connor aka, John Bourgeois, *(and if you don't get the Terminator reference, I am not sure we can*

be friends) and telling her (or me) how to destroy Skynet *(another Terminator reference).*

Truthfully, I am writing this book because it took me close to fifteen years to really start to go after my dreams. My dream. The motherload of dreams, if you want to call it that, is I am an international New York Times bestselling author. I have wanted to be an author from a young age. I loved writing. I loved getting lost in the creative element and lost in the worlds I would create.

Plus, my grandmother, or as I called her, my Nana, was one of my idols. She was this beautiful, fiery red-headed, freckled, Irish woman who loved life, loved people, loved to laugh, and could light up any room she walked into.

And she loved to write. She was an author. Sadly, though, she never published any of her work, even though it was one of her dreams. It wasn't until twenty years later that the family finally published her work, but at that point, my Nana would never see the opportunity for her work to go to print.

I tell you this because growing up, I had the imagination of a Steve Spielberg or George Lucas. Oftentimes, I would get lost in the world of my Mutant Ninja Turtles action figures as they battled out the fate of the world against their evil nemesis, Shredder. You couple that with the fact that I looked up to my Nana, and there you have it, I wanted to be a writer.

But I snuffed the dream out. I put it on the back burner. I hid it away. Hoping, praying that one day, someday, I would be an author.

So maybe, just maybe, that's why you picked up this book. Maybe you are tired of hiding your dreams. Maybe you have hidden it for so long that it is bursting to come out of you, and maybe you are trying to figure out just how to make that happen.

Well, I can tell you this, if you apply what I wish I had applied fifteen years ago, if you implement what I have learned, if you make note of where I have struggled, and if you use what I have had to add into my own life to catch my own dreams, then I promise you, you will be able to turn your dream into reality.

But first, what the heck is a "Dreamcatcher…" and what's "Dreamcatching?"

1

What the Heck is a 'Dreamcatcher' & What's 'Dreamcatching?'

Oh padawan, now, you are asking the right question. Let me explain.

When we talk about a Dreamcatcher or about Dreamcatching, we are not talking about the Native American woven net or web that was used to catch evil spirits while you slept.

We also are not talking about the Stephen King book, later turned into a movie, where four children acquire telepathic powers.

So, if any of those are your references of a Dreamcatcher or Dreamcatching, I am going to ask you to erase the board, turn the page, and delete everything you know.

Now that we cleared that out of the way let's explain what we are talking about.

When I use the word Dreamcatcher or Dreamcatching, I am speaking in the simplest terms of explaining someone who has learned the ability to catch their dreams.

And that's a key phrase that I want you to underline and go back and reread.

A Dreamcatcher is someone who has LEARNED the ABILITY to catch their dreams.

Let me explain a little further.

You ever met someone that just seemed to have it all together. I don't mean they were good at one thing. I mean, they literally had the whole package.

The type of person I am talking about isn't the one-hit-wonder boy band type of person that you later see and are like, "what happened to you."

No, I am talking about the type of person that says they are going to accomplish something (*oftentimes, it is a LARGE feat that utterly seems impossible,*) and yet somehow, someway, they seem to accomplish it.

That's a Dreamcatcher, and they have learned the art of Dreamcatching, or simply, how to catch a dream.

You've found a Dreamcatcher when one of the first things that comes to mind when you hear them say something is, "well, if there is anyone that can do it, _____, sure will figure out a way to."

That's a Dreamcatcher.

Oftentimes, the odds can be stacked against them. It might be something that has never been done before. Many times, they do not have the resources necessary to accomplish the goal. Their backs are quite often up against the wall. They are down and out, and many times the bets are hedged against them.

A perfect example of a Dreamcatcher, and I hate to say it, as a Colts fan, is Tom Brady. Like I said, I hate to say it. Tom has kicked the Colts out of the Super Bowl too many times for me to count.

But he is constantly doing things that no one has ever been able to do. You can get down to the 4th quarter, 2 minutes left in the game, Brady can be down 20 points, and the first thought that comes to mind is, "Well, if anyone can come back from this, Tom sure can."

That's a Dreamcatcher.

Another perfect example is Kevin Hart. I look up to this man even though I am 5'8" when I'm wearing my dress shoes.

He's launching a new movie, going on a global comedy tour, running a 5k in every city he's in, and he is launching his own movie production company.

"Well, if anyone can do it, Kevin sure can."

That's a Dreamcatcher.

I think you are getting the point, but I am going to drive it home just a little further.

Dwayne Johnson, another one of my idols, not just because of his movies, but because of his insane work ethic.

You hear that he is waking up and working out two times before everyone else has even rolled over and hit the snooze button.

He's launching a movie, partnering with an athletic company, launching his own tequila, and he is returning back to wrestling for a guest appearance.

"WELL, IF ANYONE CAN DO IT, DWAYNE SURE CAN."

That's a Dreamcatcher.

The problem is our society has put Dreamcatchers on a pedestal. Instead of being ordinary people who are doing amazing things. We have labeled them extraordinary people who are just doing normal things for extraordinary people.

And that thinking, let's us off the hook. We start thinking that we can't do those things because we are 'normal' people. Normal people don't catch their dreams. Normal people settle for their lot in life, and unlike Oliver Twist, never ask for more.

Well, I am here to tell you, that's bullshit. *(And excuse my French... but my last name is Bourgeois)*

The truth is whether it is Elon Musk, Oprah, Mark Cuban, Beyonce, or anyone else you can think of, these are normal people who have discovered what it takes to turn a dream into reality.

It is a skillset. It is an artform. It is a trait that anyone can learn if they put the time and effort into it.

And this book is here to show you exactly how to start doing that.

2

Now That We Know What a Dreamcatcher is, What's It Not?

Here's the sad truth. Like I mentioned in the previous chapter, Dreamcatching is a skill set that can be acquired. It can be learned. Anyone and everyone can become a Dreamcatcher, but the truth is, most won't.

And for me, that is tougher to swallow than a spoonful of cinnamon in a desert with no map to civilization.

Okay, a little extreme on the analogy, but I wanted to make my point.

You see, I have a savior complex. I want to save everyone. But not everyone wants to be saved. In some cases, Rose stays on the raft, and although there is plenty of room for Jack to row to safety, he is going to let go of Rose's hand and slip into the icy waters of the Atlantic, and you're going to bawl your eyes out (That's a Titanic movie reference for any of my 'born after the 90s' readers who didn't know. And it's also a spoiler alert. The Titanic sinks.)

Here's the good news. At any moment, both you and anyone that you know can make the decision to shift, pivot, and move into Dreamcatching and into becoming a Dreamcatcher.

So, before we talk about how to become a Dreamcatcher, let's point out the elephants in the room. Let's look at the villains of this story. The guys you have to look out for. The Lex Luthor to Superman. The Joker to Batman. The Sinestro to Green Lantern.

We know who a Dreamcatcher is, but what's it not?

Great question, Watson.

When we speak about dreams, there are three different types of dreamers. First, there are the Dreamcatchers, and we will dive into them later.
Then there are Daydreamers, and there are Dreamchasers. Each one has the dream, but each one DOES something different with that dream, and that is the key defining piece of the equation, the doing.

You see, for the majority of my life, I was a Daydreamer. I was famous for it. Both in school and outside of school, and to be honest, it got me in trouble a lot.

I grew up the eldest child with two younger twin sisters, and although I tried many more times than not to engage them in an epic battle of swords and war, they were more interested in playing "bosom buddies" with each other and setting up their pretend house.

Snore and bore if you ask me.

And there may or may not have been a certain time when my sisters were not playing as I saw fit, and I somehow convinced them to stick their fingers into a beehive, unbeknownst to them.

That's not the worst part.

I had a bat. Yeah, and I swung that bat. I dropped that bat. Screamed, "RUN," and left my sisters' fingers stuck in a beehive to fend for themselves.

Real classy, big brother stuff.

So, needless to say, having to play often by myself and being left to my own imagination was something I was very familiar with. I mean, can you blame my sisters for not wanting to play?

The problem is that being a Daydreamer during playtime activity is fine. What is not okay was that it began to carry over into my real-life dreams and into my aspirations.

So, what is A Daydreamer?

Well, let me define a Daydreamer for you. A Daydreamer lives in their very own, self-created, fantasy world. They have the dream. They know in 'theory' what they want or what sounds good. They can tell you all about it. They can describe it in vivid color, but that is it. They can come out of the dream as quickly as they go into it.

A Daydreamer often wears the dream like a badge of honor. They can tell you all about it. Daydreamers love to walk around with the dream and talk about how it is going to happen 'someday.'

But when you start to dive a little deeper, you start to realize that for some reason, life has it "out" to get these Daydreamers.

There is always a reason why they haven't started. There is always a new excuse for them. They are always waiting. Never taking action. Always stalling.

Daydreamers talk a lot. They talk and talk and talk and talk.

Think of them as a painter, but without a brush, or any paint, or a canvas, just words to describe what they are 'going' to paint. They can describe the dream, and you can live it with them, but they will never make anything of it.

They are like the 5-year-old kid on Halloween. They look the part. They act the part. They are in full costume and character. They might even sound like the character they are dressed up as, but at some point, sorry to tell ya, kid, the costume has to come off, and we have to put away the Halloween candy.

That's a Daydreamer. Sound like anyone you know?

Hey, it's okay if it sounds like the person you see regularly in the mirror.

Why?

Because daydreaming is not a chronic disease that hasn't got a cure.

Remember the whole reason I have written this book is so that I could jump in the DeLorean and sit down over a game of Street Fighter and help younger John become a Dreamcatcher.

And since that's not going to happen anytime soon, I want to help you become the Dreamcatcher that you are meant to be.

So we have talked about a Daydreamer.

But what is a Dreamchaser?

These guys can be tough to spot, but I want to point them out for you.

The reason that they are tough to spot is they often resemble a Dreamcatcher. These are the guys that give Dreamcatchers a bad name.

At some point, the Dreamchaser has moved from being a Daydreamer and has started to take action. The problem is they do not know who they are or truly what they want, so they are often swayed by outside opinion or thought.

A Dreamchaser has got the classic 'shiny object' syndrome. They are not confident in themselves or in their dream. They are taking a lot of action and putting in a lot of work. But more times than not, they end up giving up on the dream, finding a 'new' dream, being swayed by what pop culture tells them to do, and listening to everyone and anyone who doesn't believe in their idea.

Dreamchasers love to give up when the going gets tough.

Think of a Dreamchaser like you would a dog that is chasing his tail. He is exerting a lot of energy, but he is going around in circles, violently chasing his tail and breaking all of mom's furniture. He's going nowhere, like a hamster on a wheel.

I had a black cat like this growing up by the name of Ebony, and one of my favorite games to play with him was laser tag. We had this small laser pointer, back when that was what all the cool kids had, and Ebony loved that thing.

The problem is, unlike the flies that he would catch on a regular basis and devour, the laser pointer was a constant and endless frustration for Ebony.

It didn't matter how stealth, or how fast, or how agile, or how quick, or how smart Ebony was, he was never going to catch the laser and enjoy the satisfaction of consuming it.

And like clockwork, after hours of fun for me (probably more like minutes but go with me on this), Ebony would finally tire out, give up on the laser, get frustrated, and move on, only to lunge out of his hiding spot, moments later, when he was ready to go at it all over again.

That's a Dreamchaser.

And the problem with a Dreamchaser is if they are not careful, they will begin to believe that 'dreams' never become reality and that those that do catch their dreams are an 'anomaly.'

When I moved from being a Daydreamer to being a Dreamchaser, this was one of the hardest things for me because as a Dreamchaser, you tire yourself out, and then you start to build a belief that you cannot achieve your dreams and that there is something wrong with you for two reasons:

1. Because you have a dream, and dreams are stupid.

    And…

2. You must not be good enough because you can't do what Dreamcatchers are able to do.

Well, I am here to tell you that's Horse shit, with a capital H, and that's why I have written this book because I don't care where you find yourself at the moment.

A Daydreamer.

A Dreamchaser.

A "I used to be a Dreamcatcher, then I caught my dream, and now I don't know what to do."

The beautiful thing about Dreamcatching is that you can pick it up at any moment. You can brush it off. You can wipe off the cobwebs. You can make the decision to see your dreams come true.

That's what this book is here for you to do. It's here to show you how.

Imagine a large, extravagant dream, the type of dream you'd been chasing for a while but just couldn't seem to catch. Now, imagine how different your world would be if you finally caught your dream. What would that do for your family? What would that do for your legacy? What would that do for you financially? What would that do for your life as a whole?

That's what this book is here to teach you.

But first, let's talk about the secret sauce of Dreamcatching.

3

The Secret Sauce... shh don't tell anyone

I am a foodie. I'll admit it.

"Hi, I am John, and I am a foodaholic."

"Hi, John."

I always have been. It's one of the reasons I love traveling the world. It allows me to try all the different types of cuisines and to experience all the different types of flavors.

And on top of that, I love to cook. There is something about it that is extremely therapeutic for me, something in the having nothing, throwing this and that together, and "voila," "Bob's your uncle," "there you have it," a dish is created.

I grew up in a family of self-proclaimed cooks. However, none of us, besides my Memaw, were truly masters in the kitchen.

[Sorry, Dad, if you're reading this, I am including you in this mix. You make a mean steak, but if I asked

you to whip up a fettuccine from nothing, but what was
in the kitchen, Memaw would put us under the table.]

My grandmother was one of those types that when
you walked into the kitchen, it became her set, her stage,
her performance, her element.

I used to love watching her in the kitchen, whipping
up dishes from nothing. It was truly a work of art. She
would always start out with a little bit of this and a little
bit of that, and the next thing you knew, she had created
a 5-course meal.

My memaw would spend hours in the kitchen
getting dinner ready for the family. Growing up, I was
always so excited to visit her, not just because of the food
but because it was amazing to watch her be a master in
the kitchen.

And one of the things I learned, from sitting
courtside to her all-star performance, was every dish had
a "secret sauce."

Ah, the secret sauce. The ingredient that every chef
and every cook has that they never release to the public.

That one ingredient that if everyone knew what it
was, they would instantly be able to make their food taste
as good if not better than their favorite restaurant.

Truth be told, my Memaw somehow had the innate
ability to try a meal at a restaurant and then be able to

recreate it and make it even better back in her own kitchen.

It might have been the aged bacon grease that she would reuse for every meal, or that she made every dish from scratch, but whatever it was, something in her kitchen, always made her food taste so much better than everyone else's.

I remember when I got older, I asked her for her recipes for some of my favorite dishes, and although she hand wrote every recipe when I tried to reduplicate her masterpiece, it just didn't have that "secret" Memaw ingredient needed to make the dish taste the way it should.

Your dreams are no different than my Memaw's recipes.

In order for you to move away from your daydreaming, dreamchasing days, and move into becoming a Dreamcatcher and catching your dreams, you HAVE to know what that secret sauce is; that special, secret ingredient you have been missing all along.

You have to know what it is that makes the art of Dreamcatching different from all the rest, and if you don't know what that is, you won't be able to reduplicate the success that you have seen the greats accomplish.

But you already knew that. That's why you picked up this book. That's why you are reading these words.

Well, pull up a seat. I'm gonna give you the SECRET SAUCE

But here's the truth about that "secret sauce" that you might not be ready to hear:

Too often, we lose track of the most important thing necessary to making our dreams a reality. We neglect it. We turn away from it. We seek out some other answer when it has been staring us in the face the entire time.

And before you can read any further into this book, before you can look for the rest of the secrets to unlocking your dreams and your potential, you have to understand this:

YOU ARE THE SECRET SAUCE.

Wait... What???

John, you can't just drop that on us like a classic M. Night Shyamalan movie, where you see dead people, and Bruce Willis has been dead the entire time.

But it's the truth. If you want to know the answer, if you want to know the real difference it takes to making your dreams happen, then you have to understand, you are the one and only one who will make your dreams come true.

No one else. No magic bullet. No secret recipe. No fairy godmother. No one but you.

You are the most important piece to this puzzle, and you have to start there. You have to. I can teach you all the tricks, all the hacks, all the habits, all the routines, but if you do not understand that you are the key to your dreams, then none of it works.

It's kinda like the scene in the Matrix, when Neo realizes that he is "the one," and he has been "the one" the entire time. He didn't need one more karate class, one more bending the spoon moment, one more session with Morpheus and The Oracle. He had it all in him the entire time.

The same is true for you and your dreams.

But I get it. I really do. I went years thinking that I was missing something. Like everyone else had the answer, and they were just keeping it from me. I looked high and low. I read the books. I listened to the audio. I went to the seminars. I took the notes.

The common thing that I kept hearing over and over again was that strategies and techniques can be taught, but the key to truly catching your dreams and desires, is first believing that you can.

That's where it starts.

Hold up! Give me a break! You mean to tell me that my dreams rely on me believing that I can!

Yes. That's exactly what I am saying.

And for some reason, for a lot of us, that is a hard struggle. Somewhere along our journey from kid to adult, we picked up this notion that we weren't good enough or we were broken, or that we needed someone or something to make us complete.

I am right there with you. I'll be the first to admit it. This was a huge struggle for me. I grew up in a highly religious environment, constantly believing that I was not worthy. I grew up thinking I would never be good enough. I grew up keeping a track record of all my failings, all my shortcomings, all my screw-ups, and every time I had a success, I was looking around the corner for when I was going to strike out again.

Even now, as I write this, if I really wanted to, I could bring up a list of things from when I was little to now that I have messed up on.

I did not believe in myself, and because of it, I got into bad partnerships, wrong relationships and followed worthless advice because I did not understand who I was, my worth, and what I brought to the table.

So, when I heard Dreamcatchers say over and over again, that I first had to believe in myself, I did not want to listen. I knew they were lying and just weren't telling me something.

But the truth is that is where we have to start. We have to start with you first.

You are going to be the only one who spurs you on. No one else.

When the going gets tough, you are going to have to fuel your dreams because no one else will. When no one else believes, or when no one else can see what you can see, you are going to have to have the vision. When you are going against the grain and no one else can understand why, you are going to have to know what it is all about and why you are doing it.

And there we have it. When we're talking about dreaming, catching your dreams, or becoming a Dreamcatcher, that is the foundation. That is where it all begins. We can't build the house without it.

It's tough to hear. I know. Especially when the rest of the world wants to assume it's not that easy. The rest of the world wants to assume there has to be something different when it comes to making things happen.

Like an old 90s cheat code that you searched on "AskJeeves.com," printed and followed to the T so you could get unlimited lives.

Up, Down, Up, Down, Down, X, A, B, Up, Up, Down, Up.

What… No, I didn't do that... you did!!!!

Okay, let me explain it this way cause I know I am getting some pushback like:

"John, we've heard this before. That's NO SECRET SAUCE. Give us the REAL secret."

Let me explain it like this.

Growing up, my dad had his very own version of the "secret sauce." It was his secret ingredient that he would break out every summer, and every summer, I would look forward to it.

The funny thing is my dad was born and raised on the border of Louisiana and Texas, and where he is from, his secret ingredient is no secret at all. It's a staple, like pepper and salt, like butter and milk, like sugar and spice. But growing up where I was raised, his secret ingredient made all the difference for our summer feasts.

Here's what you have to know before we go any further into this story. It will give you some light on my childhood.

You need to understand that I grew up on a little island in the middle of the Pacific, called Guam, and when I say island, I want you to think about it in the traditional sense.

Palm trees. Coconuts. Beaches. Waves.
We're talking "Survivor Season 1" style island.

It literally takes an hour to get around the whole thing and is only 9 miles wide by 30 miles long. At its thinnest point, you can get across the island in 15 minutes.

We're talking about year-round sunshine. Ripe mango trees. Hula dancing, grass skirts, and beautiful sandy shores.

An Island.

And growing up, my family would always take a family adventure every summer, somewhere off the island.

One of our many family getaways was to an island just south of Guam, about an hour flight, called Yap.

Yap is absolutely beautiful. It is untouched. The people still live off the land, and somehow, it has remained an island lost in time.

Now, one of the things that I can always remember about our getaways to Yap was the FAMOUS crab boils that we would always have.

This wasn't your normal crab boil. To begin with, as kids, we were given the task to catch dinner, and in Yap, this isn't done with a net or cage or running down to the local fish market and purchasing yourself some Alaskan King crab.

No. In Yap, you catch crabs with your bare hands.

Yes. You read that correctly. You catch them with your bare hands.

So, if you are ever stranded on a deserted island, not knowing what to do, you'll want to read this next part carefully and closely:

There's a trick to catching crabs with your bare hands. The first thing you have to understand is that crabs follow the sun. So, when you find a crab hole wherever the sun is, is where the crab is facing.

What that means for the kids or anyone else trying to catch these crabs is that you are reaching your hand into the sand from the opposite direction of the sun, down another crab hole, and pulling the crabs out of their lair.

We would fill buckets upon buckets of crabs when we were done, and we were ready to feast.

Now, like I mentioned, this wasn't your normal crab boil. Not only had the kids caught these crabs by hand, but there was a special ingredient that made these boils so good.

And here is where I am going to share with you a FAMILY ingredient so you too can go to a deserted island and have your own crab boil.

The thing that made my dad's crab boils so good was the fact that he added into the crab boil "*Louisiana Crawfish, Shrimp & Crab Boil*" seasoning.

A seasoning that if you lived in Louisiana, you could pick up at your local supermarket.

That's it. That's what made it so special. That's what made it taste so good. But if you lived on a small island in the middle of the ocean, that seasoning made all the difference.

So, what's a crab boil and "*Louisiana Crawfish, Shrimp & Crab Boi*l" seasoning got to do with you catching your dream?

Everything.

You see, if you knew you could replicate my dad's famous summer feasts by just ordering the seasoning online, adding it to water, and kicking up your feet to a nice Bud Light, you'd already be having dinner.

The problem is. Most of the world, your daydreamers and dreamchasers, don't understand this. They view my dad's famous boils as if it was made from a sweet nectar created from the gods.

But the secret was it was a store-bought box, mixed into water, and before you knew it, you were 'enjoying yourself a good 'ole fashion Cajun boil.'

Well, you are that ***Louisiana Crawfish, Shrimp & Crab Boil* seasoning.**

We just have to add you to your dreams in order to make the magic happen.

So, if you're the key to your dreams, how do we start believing that and begin catching our dreams?

4

It's Time to Discover Your Cape and Step into Your Superhero

The problem is not that there is something wrong with you. The problem is you don't believe in the true form that you were created and destined to be. That's the real problem.

In order for you to be a Dreamcatcher and start catching your dreams, you have to know who you are and be able to stand tall in that and walk in that. The problem is we came out of the womb confident in who we are, but most of us won't die that way.

I love superhero stories. I always have. It's something as a boy that I always wished that I could be. It was probably because I was an 80s baby, and Saturdays were my favorites. After the chores, I would race over to the TV, and with my bowl of breakfast, I'd throw on my morning cartoons. Some of my favorites were Batman, X-Men, and of course, Superman.

Superman was one of my all-time favorites, and not because of the flight or superhuman strength or any of the other obvious reasons. It wasn't because of his superspeed or his laser eyes, or even his freezing breath.

No, the reason that I loved Superman was because of his origin story.

Man, oh man, I loved his origin story, and if you are not a comic book or superhero cartoon fan, you will not know Superman's origin story. So, real quick, without me having to give you a long-winded Saturday morning cartoons tutorial, let me explain Superman's origin story.

You see, Superman, at one point, was a little babe. He grew up on a distant planet that was completely destroyed, and as the planet was entering annihilation, his parents decided to save their only boy. They put him in a rocket ship and sent him off to another planet. That planet being Earth.

Now Superman didn't step into the red cape and large "S" on his chest when he arrived. No, it was the exact opposite. He crash-landed onto Earth as a baby boy. With all the needs of a child. Having no clue who he was and what he was capable of, and he was discovered by a small-town farming couple who raised him as their own.

Here's the part about Superman that I love.

Superman was raised as a human. He was given the restrictions of a human. He was given the restraints of gravity. He was given the limitations of being a small-town farm boy who would never amount to anything of significance.

And it is through Superman's origin story that he has to come to understand who he truly is, what he is truly capable of, and what his true calling really is.

The entire way on that journey, it is a struggle for him.

Why? Because from a child, he was convinced that he was nothing special. Of no significance. That he was to husk the corn and mow the lawn.

Now, I know what you are asking...

What does Superman and Dreamcatching or being a Dreamcatcher have to do with anything?

And my answer. It has everything to do with it.

Your story is the EXACT same origin story as Superman's. You may not believe it at the moment, but it is. Let me prove it to you.

The sole fact that you are here on this planet, reading this book, proves that you too are on your own "superhero in disguise" journey.

How can I say that? Well, there was a trillion to one odds of you existing and you stepping into this world. You read that correctly. A trillion to one odds of it being Susie or Freddie reading this book, and mommy and daddy having someone else as their child, but instead, here you are.

Did you know that you have better odds of winning the lottery than you do of being born?

Let's not stop there.

Did you know that the female body does everything it possibly can to not conceive?

That's right. Mommy's body tried everything it possibly could to try to make sure that nine months later, you weren't screaming, and crying, and wanting some milk.

Did you know that in order for you to come into existence, you had to be the fastest, you had to be the strongest, you had to be the most persistent and resilient, or you would have lost your chance of existence?

I don't care what you see in the mirror right now. I don't care what you have been told or how many failings you have had in the past.

Your story is the same as Superman. You just haven't discovered who you truly are, but the good news is. You will. That's why you picked up this book, and that's why I am writing it.

You see as a child. We were near invincible. We knew we could do it all. We knew we were the fastest or the smartest. We would attempt to draw a circle, show it to mommy and daddy, and we knew we were the next Picasso.

But somewhere along the way, we accepted the notion that this wasn't the truth and that this wasn't our story. Instead of putting on the cape and the large S, we started to believe the lies that were fed to us that we weren't good enough, that we weren't worthy enough, that if it has never been done before, then it can never be done, and therefore, you should never even try.

I am here to tell you that every one of us is a superhero.

I am also here to tell you that most of us, the daydreamers and dreamchasers, will never discover that superhero. They will slip off into oblivion, never knowing how powerful they truly were.

And what's even worse is that instead of discovering how amazing we are, how unstoppable we can be, how invincible we were made to be, instead of stepping into our superhero and embracing it, the majority of those around us take our so-called "limitations," and wear them as a badges of honor.

- I can't
- I don't know how
- I'm not smart enough
- I don't have the money
- I never went to college
- I am not creative enough
- No one in my family ever has
- I don't come from the right part of town
- No one has ever done it before
- I tried, and I failed, so it's not for me
- I am too young
- I am too old
- I am too fat
- I am too skinny

Instead of embracing our superhero, we choose to embrace our supervillain, and we let that "supervillain" define who we are.

Really? That's what you are going to do. A trillion to one odds, and that's who you choose to embrace.

Here's what you have to understand.

By embracing your supervillain limitations, you begin to create a false reality. A reality where you seek out evidence that you "aren't smart" or that you "don't have enough money" or that you "are too old." And in seeking out the evidence, the old adage becomes true "seek, and you will find." You end up finding the evidence that solidifies your supervillain limitations.

It's called a self-fulfilling prophecy.

But I am here to tell you that as easy as it is to put on your supervillain and find the evidence of why you "can't" achieve your dreams, it's just as easy to put on your superhero and discover all the amazing ways to achieve your dreams.

So how do we move from the supervillain *'limiting'* version of yourself to your superhero **limitless** version?

The Art of Dreamcatching

5

What's the Worst Thing to Drink Out Of? A Dirty Glass, Of Course!!!

When it comes to Dreamcatching, we must first start by making sure we are rinsing out the glass before we continue forward with the dream.

I don't know about you, but when I was growing up, my house was a little different than everyone else's. I was raised in a home that was more geared towards the 1950s versus the 1990s, and my parents were firm believers that if you lived in the house, you cleaned the house.

And we aren't talking about a $20 an hour cleaning service charge that I'd tack on at the end of the month. No. If we lived there, it meant we cleaned there, and we cleaned there for free.

One of our 1950s family traditions, if you want to call it that, was to eat together as a family. My dad would get home from work, and my mom would serve up dinner. We'd sit around the table and chat about our day and have a grand old time together.

At the end of it, we would clear off the table. Take the dishes into the kitchen, and we would have to wash the dishes by hand.

I am talking, warm water, add your soap, rinse, wash, and repeat. No dishwasher. All by hand.

Every night without fail.

It was one of those tasks that my siblings and I regularly rotated, but there was one night that I got given the ultimate task.

<u>Inspect my younger sister's work.</u>

AND OH, DID I INSPECT IT.

I came into the kitchen like Inspector Gadget, magnifying glass and all, looking for that one spec of dirt on any glass. Sure, I could have been a little more lenient with her, but there was a rule on the line that if you did not execute the dinner dishes well that night, it meant you had to be on them for the next night.

And the next night was my night, so there was no way I wasn't finding some sort of dirt particle on my sister's dishes. I'd plant the evidence if I had to.

All kidding aside, I am going to be frank with you. I am pretty sure my sister gave up trying to do the dishes at some point because she was on dinner dish duty for over a year, and that meant good 'ole older brother was her judge and jury for a solid year too.

I look back on those evenings and laugh. Obviously, part of the reason I laugh is because I was definitely not the nicest older brother to my sisters sometimes.

And sis, if you're reading this, I am so sorry. I was definitely an ass!

But I also look back on those evenings and am so thankful for them.

Why?

Because it taught me a valuable lesson that I would not have learned if I was not responsible for dinner dishes when it came to my night.

I don't know about you, but anytime I have guests over now and offer them a glass of wine or water to drink, I always check to make sure the glass is clean.

I do the eye check. You know what that one is. You look around the glass to make sure that there's no crud from the night before. I sometimes even do the smell check and rinse out the cup, just in case.

The weird thing is we do that for our guests when it's time to pour them a drink. We want our guests to have the best of the best.

But we do not do that for ourselves on a daily, weekly, monthly basis when it comes to our dreams and especially when it comes to our mental fortitude.

*If you are going to step into your superhero **limitless** version and start to become a Dreamcatcher, you HAVE to discover what I call "The Art of Rinsing Out the Glass."*

Let's be honest. Dreaming is stressful. Dreaming is not for the faint of heart. It isn't for the weak. It isn't for the weary. Dreaming, and specifically, Dreamcatching, is hard work.

It takes a lot of effort to day in and day out, to turn your dreams into reality. Many times, you have to do it in the face of opposition, in the face of defeat, in the face of all the odds stacked against you.

Why do you think so many people are either Daydreamers or Dreamchasers? Because they have not learned what it takes to turn their dreams into reality and to catch them.

That's not you.

How do I know? Because you picked up this book. Because you have read this far. You, a Dreamcatcher, are doing everything you can to learn how to catch your dreams.

And I applaud you for that, but I must share with you that the first step to catching your dreams is learning how to rinse out your glass, how to strengthen your mindset, how to set your resolve for the road ahead.

We, as Dreamcatchers, love watering the dream. We love turning the impossible into the possible. We love putting in the work and getting the results. We love being able to care for others and helping them succeed. We love bringing value. We love all the components of catching the dream.

But so often, we neglect ourselves on the road to catching our dreams.

And that is the most important part of YOUR dream. No one else is going to catch YOUR dream. No one else is going to care as much about YOUR dream as you do. No one else is going to put in the time and attention into YOUR dream as you will.

Why? Because it's <u>YOUR</u> dream.

Which is why YOU are such a vital piece to the equation. Without you, your dream does not live on. If you burn out, if you give up, if you throw in the towel, your dream dies with you.

I cannot tell you how many people I have seen burn out, give up, roll over, pull the covers over their head, and go back to bed just because they chose to neglect themselves.

I have seen peers do it. I have seen celebrities do it. I have seen mentors do it. I have seen coaches do it.

Heck! There have been days and moments when I did it or wanted to do it myself.

And that is why learning how to rinse out your own glass is so important.

You must learn how to rinse out your own glass before you start to fill up everyone else's glasses. You must learn how to focus on you rather than focusing on everyone else, first and foremost.
Too many times, we want to focus on everything else and everyone else, and we forget about ourselves along the way.

A Dreamcatcher, one who has learned how to rinse out their glass before they begin to serve others or even serve their dream, is a Dreamcatcher who will be able to weather the storms of life when the storms start coming.

A healthy you is a healthy dream. A nourished you is a nourished dream. A thriving you is a thriving dream.

As a child, I was a very active kid. Like I mean active. Like we are talking hyperactive. I probably could have been classified as ADHD. That's how bad I was, but to me, I just loved life and had a lot of energy.

It made it especially interesting for my parents and my sisters because I was always "go go go" until I crashed and then started it all over again.

On top of that, I had an insatiable curiosity and a willingness to try anything and everything. And a willingness to win. I loved risk. I loved the rush. I loved the adrenaline. I loved the experience of trying out something new and extreme. You can only imagine that I was the kid that your dad said, "Don't do that…" and before he could finish his sentence, it was done. I had already done what he was advising me not to do, and in most cases, I had injured myself somehow or injured someone else.

I have had my share of concussions, broken bones, stitches, and scars for the both of us. I promise you that.

One of those moments just so happened to be when no one else was around to advise me not to proceed any further. I was at my own risk. Man, would I have to pay for that.

Every summer, we would leave the island and experience a "new world." Probably in part because my parents loved building amazing memories, and probably in part because they needed to get me out of the house, or I'd destroy something.

One of our many adventures was off to an amazing place called Bali. It was beautiful and to this day still is. I can still remember the white sandy beaches, the friendly locals, and the crazy monkeys. Oh, the crazy monkeys.

It was definitely a vacation for the books for many different reasons, including this story.

What you have to understand about Bali, though, at least at the time of this trip, was that it was not your first-world country. Sure, the tourist strip was westernized and extremely modernized, but the rest of the country was dirt roads, rice patties, and make-shift huts. I mean, they still rode elephants for transportation, so you have to understand that not everything was clean, hygienic, or completely Kosher.

On this particular day, my family and I woke up and had a beautiful breakfast overlooking the ocean.

I can still remember the watermelon cubes they served us for breakfast, so fresh and so sweet.

Oh my gosh. Take me back. My mouth is watering just thinking about it.

Generally, our vacations were jammed packed with activities, but for some reason, on this day, my parents hadn't planned any special outings, and that was perfect for me. All I wanted to do was spend the entire day jumping in and out of the pool while enjoying all the entertaining games the hotel had set up for kids. I don't remember much more of the day, except for the fact that I was exhausted by the end of it, extremely hungry, and in an especially feisty mood by the time dinner rolled around.

That evening my parents had decided that we would venture out of the hotel and visit a local restaurant in town. As my sisters and I exited our taxi, my sisters commented on the restaurant's water fountain and assumed that it must be chlorine water since we spent the entire day poolside, in and out of chlorine.

Well, as only an older brother can do, I assessed the situation, saw that the fountain was not running, and decided to argue with them and tell them that they were wrong. Like I said, typical older brother.

Now, if you know anything about sibling relations, you know they do not like to be told they are wrong, and my sisters and I were no different. Our argument somehow, someway proceeded to get to the point where these words came out of my mouth, "No, you are wrong. That is not a chlorine pool. See."

And at that exact moment, I bent down, scooped up a handful of water, swigged it around in my mouth, spat it out, and thought nothing of it.

Oh, was I wrong.

I paid dearly for that argument with my sisters. It wasn't at dinner. It wasn't even that first evening.

Sure, I tossed and turned a bit and woke up hot as hell. Yeah, I didn't feel the greatest at breakfast and was sweating like a hog, but that isn't where I paid for my mistake.

I paid for my mistake on the amazing excursion that my parents had planned the following day. We were going to be visiting the monkey temples of Bali. If you are not familiar with Bali, you will have no clue what this is or why as a young boy, even not feeling the greatest, I had to go.

The monkey temples of Bali are where the Balinese have dedicated a place of worship, but because they revere monkeys in their culture and in their religion, the monkeys have been allowed to roam, nest, and visit with any and all tourists that come to view these temples.

If you ever venture over to Bali and decide to visit the monkey temples, the tourist guide will warn you before your visit these temples that you must remove any jewelry, leave your glasses and sunglasses in the car, and hide your wallets and purses because these monkeys are famous for playing nice and then stealing anything they can get their hands on.

That morning, because the plan was to spend most of the day at the monkey temples, feeding them, and watching them play, the family got a quick breakfast at McDonald's, and I got a cup of water. That was all I was hungry for.

Why? Well, because I wasn't feeling so hot and because the night before, I had had a swig of unchlorinated third-world water.
You wouldn't be hungry either.

All was fine as we entered the monkey temple. I watched as my sisters fed the bananas to the monkeys and was enjoying myself. Holding onto my McDonald's water cup as if it was a comfort blanket, I was just observing the tourists and the monkeys interact.

54

The monkeys were jumping from tree to tree, playing, eating, tackling the smaller monkeys, and loving life.

All was fine. Until one lone monkey, the smaller of the pack, began to approach me as I was sitting on the wall. This had never been the plan. My parents knew I wasn't feeling so well, so they had not given me any food to feed the monkeys with.

I was there just to observe, but to this lone monkey, that was not good enough. He approached with caution expecting me to hand him a banana, and I just looked at him and told him I had nothing.

He slowly approached me, and I leaned onto the wall. I let him know where he could find food and tried to be as helpful as I could be. I pointed to the other tourists but let him know I was not the guy with any of the food.

I thought we had an understanding. But then, without any warning or hesitation, the runt ran at me and snagged my McDonalds water cup from my hand and stood in front of me.

He and I stared dead into each other's eyes for what felt like an eternity. And then, without a beat of the eye, this feisty little monkey tore my water in front of his 10-year-old observer and threw the cup on the ground.

That is when the fever, disease-infested, unchlorinated water decided to take its toll on me. I, an absolute animal lover and a jokester at heart, burst into tears and started repeatedly sobbing, "My water. My... wat... er...."

And it was at this point that my parents realized something was drastically wrong. I spent the rest of the trip sweating out whatever was in me, tossing and turning in the dark hotel room with the drapes closed. All while my sisters and family enjoyed the rest of the vacation.

Now, why do I share that story with you?

Because if we are not careful, if we haven't learned how to mentally stay healthy, we try to pretend that everything is fine and dandy. We put on a good face. Act out the charades. We do everything we are "supposed" to do, but when the 'monkey' of life comes along and tears up our water cup, we lose it.

6

Okay! Now, How Do We Rinse Out the Glass?

So, then the real question is, how do you start to rinse out your glass versus sobbing over your torn-up McDonald's cup?

You start by first discovering what your dream is.

<u>What is the Dream?</u>

Before you can start to catch the dream, or work on it, or action out the steps to making it happen, you have to know what the dream is.

And I don't mean one of those foggy, I just woke up and can tell you that it was an AWESOME dream, but I can't remember any of the details, and if you were to ask me in 10 minutes what the dream was about, I couldn't tell you at all.

You really have to KNOW what the dream is.

Just like understanding that you are the secret sauce in making your dream a reality, knowing "what" your dream is, is like knowing what's for dinner.

That's how important it is.

This is where many Daydreamers and Dreamchasers get it wrong. They want a "nice" house. They want the "dream" job. They want to "publish" the book. They would love to "travel." They want to make "a LOT" of money. They want to win the ring, star in the movie, paint the canvas. They want the accomplishment, but they have no detail to it.

The truth is they do not even truly know what they want.

In order to be a Dreamcatcher, you have to know the dream so well that, at times, you cannot tell what is the dream and what is reality. You have to be able to feel it. You must be able to sense the emotions within it. You must be able to see it in full color and glory. In some cases, you have to be able to smell it and touch it. The more detail to the dream that you can give it, the better.

Now, there are two amazing ways of discovering what the dream is for you: what it looks like, what it feels like, what emotions you have when it is accomplished, etc.

One of them I will share in a brief moment, but the other, I want you to do <u>right now</u>.

Like, I mean, put down the book and ACTUALLY do it. That's why you're here, right?!?

It is a very simple but such a POWERFUL exercise to do.

I want you to take out a pen and piece of paper, and I want you to write out the following statement at the top of your page:

<u>*"It Is A Year From Now & It's Been My Best Year Ever"*</u>

Then I want you to put aside all your excuses, all of the things that you '*think*' are stopping you from accomplishing your dream, and I want you to just write. Let your pen flow.

I want you to imagine that you have had the best year of your life, and I want you to write it out in full color:

- What did it look like?
- What did you do?
- Who did you do it with?
- Where did you go?
- What did you accomplish?
- What sort of money did you make?

- What have you always wanted to do that you FINALLY did?
- How'd it make you feel?

Write it out in as much color and detail as you possibly can, and then once you have done that, read it out loud with as much excitement as possible, with a smile on your face.

And then, read that out every night for a week.

That exercise that I just gave you is one that I do every quarter. It is amazing what will happen when you look back in a year and see what you have accomplished. It's like rocket fuel in propelling you into your dream.

Now that we have the dream, let's work on how we begin to rinse out your glass on a consistent, daily basis.

What I am about to share with you has worked tremendously in my life, but it has also worked amazingly in my client's lives, in the lives of the mentors that I have worked with, and the serial Dreamcatchers that I have studied and have had the chance to connect with.

But don't just take my word for it.

Test me and try it out and watch what it does for you and your dream.

As a Dreamcatcher, you are required to do the things that others won't, the sort of things that others have tried and stopped, the things that others don't want to know about when it comes to turning your dream into a reality.

That's what makes you a Dreamcatcher.

So, the things that I am about to share with you regarding rinsing out your glass are things that I want you to begin to add into your own life if you haven't already.

Here are six amazing ways to rinse out my glass on a daily basis:

1. **<u>Find A Morning Routine:</u>**

This is so powerful. I cannot stress it enough. Our lives are constantly moving, constantly going, constantly taking off. Take it from me, a dad of four kids, a Dreamcatcher, a life partner, an entrepreneur, an author, an investor, a coach. I understand that the external requirements are heavy, and this is why a morning routine is so powerful.

I personally wake up at 4am. I have a sunlight alarm that wakes me up before my alarm goes off. I drink a glass of water to start my day, and I begin to work on myself before any distractions can be thrown my way.

I would challenge you. If you have never woken up before your home does, or before the birds do, or before the kids start running around downstairs. I challenge you to start.

Your morning routine should prepare you mentally, physically, spiritually, and emotionally for the day. It's comparable to a fighter putting on his armor before battle or a boxer putting on his gloves before the fight.

Your morning routine should be exactly that for you and your day. Your morning routine is also a remarkable place to work on your dream and get you one step closer each day to accomplishing that dream.

Hear me when I say this:

You do not need to be like me and wake up at 4am.

You do not have to do exactly as I do, but you do need to find a morning routine that primes you for your day and prepares you for your dream. It is not a coincidence that many ultra-successful Dreamcatchers wake up before the sun does. Maybe, just maybe, if you want this year to be your best year ever as a Dreamcatcher, maybe, just maybe, you should start.

2. **Discover Gratitude:**

Wow.

This was and has been a game-changer for me. Before I learned gratitude and before I learned to practice it on a daily basis, I always looked at being grateful as a weakness. Like if I was thankful for a broken-down car, or my torn-up clothes, or my dead-end job, that somehow it would make me complacent, and I would settle and stop going after my dream.

And because of that, I would push off my gratefulness and my happiness until I had accomplished the goal and achieved the dream.

Here's the secret, the thing they never tell you. The thing that I want to share with you right now:

If you don't discover gratitude, in the current moment where you are today, in the moment before you 'catch' your dream, I can promise you that once you do 'catch' your dream...

You will reach your dream's pinnacle. You will get to the top. You will feel a brief moment of euphoria, and then you will ask yourself, 'is that all?' as that moment quickly slips away.

I cannot tell you how many times I have had the large audacious dream that I eventually achieved, and because I haven't discovered gratitude, I would get 'bummed' out because the emotions that I thought I would feel once I achieved the dream, lasted for a moment and then were gone.

And then it was onto the next goal or the next dream.

If you cannot be thankful for the car you have today, the Tesla is not going to change that when you get it. It will eventually turn into the minivan that you have now, and you'll have your eyes set on the next shiny object.

Here's another little secret for you, that no one wants to tell you, that I want to tell you today:

If you can learn how to be sincerely grateful, if you can learn how to truly enjoy each and every moment while you are in them, if you can figure out how to be thankful for the small things, you will not only be ecstatic when you have accomplished the dream, but you will enjoy the process along the way. When the high of catching the dream subsides, you will not crash, or get depressed, or get frustrated, or be like a "druggie" saying, "where's my next dream? I need another hit."

You'll look back on your memories, and you will be thankful that you lived in those moments, in those memories, versus trying to wish them away.

I had to learn this lesson the hard way. Several years back, before I had learned this lesson, a relationship that I was in for 13 years ended. I went from having the house, the car, the job, the friends, having it all, but never satisfied, always wanting more, always wanting it to be better.

I went from having it all to having to sleep on the floor of a 750 sq ft apartment for 8 months. No car. No furniture. No bed. Nothing.

You want to talk about learning to be thankful in the moments with what you have now?

I promise you. When you have had no couch or bed for 8 months, and finally, you do, you begin to cherish it.

To this day, there will be times during my morning routine or throughout my day where I am like, "I am so thankful for the amazing comfortable bed that I got to sleep in."

So how do we start to discover gratitude in your life without you having to hit rock bottom to discover it?

Simple.

Here are three ways for you to discover gratitude while you are rinsing out your glass:

A. Start a daily journal where you write out 3x things that you are grateful for every single day. Initially, this process will be easy. The challenge is to find three things that you are thankful for from the last 24-hour time period.

B. Spend 5 mins each day, hand over your heart, eyes closed, distractions off, going through all the things that you are thankful for. Start with being thankful for your heart and the last breath you took.

C. Find a "Gratitude Token." Pick up a small smooth rock or something else a little more fancy if you want and drop it into your pocket or purse. Every time you reach into your pocket, fellas, or ladies, go to grab your lip-gloss and touch your Gratitude Token, you have to find something in your immediate surrounding area to be thankful for.

When you start to do one of the above or even all of the above, you will be amazed at how much you went through on a daily, moment-by-moment basis, without realizing how blessed you already are, even without your dream being achieved. It's like turning on the lights and realizing just how dark it was.

3. <u>Start To Establish Who You Are Becoming Through Affirmations:</u>

I am going to be honest with you.

Growing up, I had the worst self-esteem. I was a scrawny, short, hyperactive, homeschooled, white kid growing up on an island. I stuck out like a sore thumb.

I was constantly seeking others' attention and validation, and oftentimes, because I was seeking others' validation so much, they would end up pushing me away. Which led me down the spiral of the fact I was not good enough, not worthy, couldn't be my true self, and the list goes on and on. An endless spiral and loop, simply because I was not confident in who I was.

Or more importantly:

<u>FOCUSED ON WHO I WAS BECOMING</u>

I remember my freshmen year. It was the first year that I had been allowed to go to school, like "real school." Up until then, my mom was my teacher, and my sisters were my classmates. So going to school was a pretty big deal.

I was so excited to be able to finally go to school, but the school that my parents sent me to was famous for one thing.

Their basketball team.

I mean, that is literally all they talked about, all they did, all they practiced, and clearly all they loved. The varsity basketball players were like gods in that school.

And then there's me…

Well, let's just say I am great at defense, just don't ask me to take a shot. Even with all that, I found myself a small group of friends and even found a girlfriend at the school.

Now, in my freshman year, And1(s) were what everyone was wearing. If you were wearing Nikes, you didn't know where it was at. And1(s) were in every store front window. They were sponsoring dunk competitions, and they were on every commercial. They were what all the "cool" kids had.

Well, I wasn't wearing Nikes or And1(s), and so when Christmas rolled around, I begged my parents to buy me the newest and greatest And1s. I wanted to make an impression when I got back from winter break. I begged and begged.

When Christmas arrived, sure enough, there was a box under the tree with my name on it. Neatly wrapped. The shake test confirmed it had to be shoes, and I was excited. It finally came time. The moment I had been waiting for.

I was given the box and unwrapped it, and to my surprise, I wasn't looking at And1(s), but I was looking at some really cool white and blue Payless ShoeSource pump shoes.

And I am not being sarcastic *(which I know is tough to know when I am and when I am not, so I figured I'd spell it out for you.)* I am not being sarcastic.

They weren't the And1 shoes that I wanted, but I thought they were really cool.

Now, as a kid, I could get it. I knew that the And1 shoes were like $100, and Payless ShoeSource sold "knock off wannabes" at a fifth of the cost, but I didn't care. These were awesome, and I was excited. I couldn't wait to show my friends at school my new "kicks." This was it. I was finally going to be accepted by the cool kids.

(Little Fun Fact: I just looked up And1 shoes because I was writing this chapter and was feeling all nostalgic, and they sell them at Walmart now for $11)

I remember lacing up my shoes the morning back to school. I couldn't wait. I walked into school with this new confidence in my step. This was my day. Got into class. Threw my book bag down at my desk. Sat down and was pumped to show off my new shoes.

One of the basketball varsity classmates sat down next to me and saw my shoes. He then proceeded to point and, as loud as he could say to the class, "What are those? Payless Shoes? What mommy and daddy couldn't buy you the real thing?"

And started laughing. Next thing I knew, he had a group of his friends all doing the same.

I'll tell you this. I don't remember much more of the day. Well, besides, the fact that my girlfriend happened to also dump me on the day, but other than that, all I do remember is I never wore those shoes again.

The funny thing is most of us are the exact same.

We allow our external environment, our past, our peers, our news outlets, our feeds, tell us what we can or cannot be. Instead of rocking the Payless Shoes because we like them, we hide them in the closet and shame ourselves for not being what everyone else tells us that we are meant to be.

That's not a Dreamcatcher, and that will get you nowhere close to catching your dreams.

You want to be a Dreamcatcher?

Then you have to cut that shit out. Like get up from the couch, eject the VHS, and put another VHS in that helps set you up for your dreams.

If you are going to become someone who sees only their dreams and hears no one else's noise, if you are going to become someone unstoppable and tenacious, you have to believe in yourself. You have to have a rock-solid "Payless ShoeSource" type of self-esteem that knows who you are and who you are becoming.

And here's what you need to know about self-esteem. It is built on 3 components:

- Accomplishments
- Relationships
- And most importantly, self-love.

Why do I say most importantly?

Because if you have not learned to love yourself first, you will seek out the accomplishments, and you will seek out the relationships to validate you versus you validating yourself.

You will go on this emotional roller coaster where when the accomplishments are there, and the relationships are there, it's amazing, and you are at an all-time high. But when the accomplishments are not there, and the relationships are in the "can," you will be in the depths of despair. You'll go from one accomplishment to another and one relationship to the next, hoping and praying that they will lift your self-esteem.

Newsflash: They won't, and you'll just end up buying another ticket to the roller coaster ride and do it all over again.

That's not what it takes to become a Dreamcatcher. That's a Dreamchaser at its core.

So, the question then is how do you stop seeking the accomplishments and the validations from others and start believing in you, trusting in you, and know without a shadow of doubt that you are capable of everything you have dreamed of?

You quite literally have to STOP playing your old tapes (hence the VHS reference) and start playing new ones. You have to begin to tell yourself who you are and who you are becoming versus letting everyone else do that for you or allowing your past or your failures to do that for you.

You have to <u>DECIDE</u> who you want to be and who you are becoming and start playing those tapes day in and day out until you step into that new version of you.

In the self-help world, they call these affirmations.

Quite simply, all an affirmation means is rather than calling yourself "ugly" (*which in and of itself is an affirmation; it's just a negative affirmation*), you start singing "I am so pretty" (*which is a positive affirmation*) at the top of your lungs.

Eventually, and I promise you it works 'cause I have done it in my own life and have watched it happen in others, you start to believe what you are saying, and you start to walk out what you are saying.

I promise you this:

If I had those Payless ShoeSource shoes today, you better believe I'd be rocking them everywhere I go, even in my sleep.

Now it's your turn. Time to start focusing on who you want to become.

Here are three ways for you to start establishing who you are becoming through affirmations:

A. Break out that journal and start to write out "I Am" statements. The key to this is to not write out who you are today but who you want to be in the future and who you are becoming. Make sure to have characteristics of who you are becoming and not just materialistic things.

B. Crack open Youtube and start listening to "I am affirmations" at a low decibel level where you can barely hear it. Do it while you're at work, while you're sleeping, while you're driving, do it as often as possible. It's amazing how your day will suddenly start going better when you do this. This is a game-changer.

C. Catch yourself and your negative thoughts when they decide to pop up and rewrite them with who you are becoming. The easiest way I have found to do this while in the moment is as soon as you realize you had the thought, take your pointer finger and jab it into the cuticle of your thumb nail. Then once you have done this, take the negative thought and say out loud the opposite of it.

Yes. It's going to be painful, BUT I promise you. The brain doesn't like the pain, and it will eventually stop thinking the thought because you are jabbing your cuticle every time it does.

4. <u>Visiting Your Dream Through Visualization:</u>

You ever watch any of the old news footage of Mohammad Ali back in his prime?

I have. Oh man, do I love watching those reels.

Besides being amazing at affirmations:

- *"I am the GREATEST."*
- *"I'm so fast that last night I turned off the light switch in my hotel room and was in bed before the room was dark."*
- *"Just last week, I murdered a rock, injured a stone, hospitalized a brick. I'm so mean. I make medicine sick."*

If you ever watched Mohammad, he would often announce the exact round that he was going to knock out his opponents.

And HE'D BE RIGHT ABOUT IT!!

Mohammad didn't do this just once or twice. He did it over and over again.

How?

How is it that Dreamcatchers can walk into their dream, oftentimes at the height of their nerves, and be so confident in themselves and what they are going to be accomplishing?

How can a Thomas Edison labor intensely over and over and over again until he has gotten the light bulb right?

How can Elon Musk continue to launch rockets after rockets and not want to throw in the towel when they continue to crash?

How can Walt Disney go through bankruptcy at the beginning of the Great Depression and still go on to create the happiest place on earth?

It's because they are not Daydreamers or Dreamchasers.

You see, for Daydreamers and Dreamchasers, they'll visit their dreams maybe once or twice. They'll create the scrapbook, make the vision board, write out the goal, and then they'll never revisit it again.

Dreamcatchers, on the other hand, visit the dream over and over and over and over again. They live in the dream. They see the color. They feel the emotions. They hear the sounds.

They are as much a part of their dream as their dream is a part of them, and with that comes unwavering faith, belief, and confidence in what can be done.

Why?

Because they have already been there. They have already watched the movie. They know the ending. They can tell you who did it, when the bad guy is going to pop out and try to scare you, what twists will be in the movie, where the easter eggs are in the movie. They can tell you all about it because they have watched the movie over and over and over again.

The same has to be for you. If you are going to become a Dreamcatcher and turn your dreams into a reality, you have to do the same.

So then, how do we do that?

Here are three ways for you to visit your dream through visualization:

A. Grab your journal and daily write out your dream. Write it out in such a way that it has already been accomplished. Use statements like "I am" or "I have" versus statements like "I want," "I'm going to," or "I am trying."

B. Take a moment, put on some soothing music, read your dream out loud with confidence, close your eyes, and start to imagine what that dream would look like and how it would feel. If, when you imagine the dream, it is in black and white, try to bring it to color, and if, when you imagine the dream, it already is in color, start to brighten the colors. Make the reds more red, the blues more blue, so on so forth.

C. Spend some time with your future self. Put on some soothing calm music. Close your eyes and imagine that you are meeting your 5-year future self. What would you look like? What have you accomplished? Ask them questions related to your dream. Let them tell you all about it.

I tell you. I have been writing out my dreams for a while now and spending time with them, but recently I started adding into my routine time to sit down with my 5-year future self, and it has been a remarkable experience.

5. <u>Being Still & Meditating:</u>

As a Dreamcatcher, this is a must. We live in such a fast pace, constantly moving, chaotic world. Everyone is talking. Everyone is pulling for our attention.

You are constantly being inundated with new information and old information. Whether that be the soda company that wants you to buy their product or the new show that is begging you to stream it, or quite frankly, the little minion at your ankles that won't stop asking for an ice cream cone.

We are being pulled at from every direction, and the crazy thing is if we turned off all of that noise, our minds would still be shouting at us and pulling at us.

Letting us know that we have to pay this bill, that we need to pick this item up from the grocery store, that we need to reach out to that friend and wish them a 'Happy Birthday.'

We are constantly on the move, constantly going, constantly doing.

To be honest. The more technologically advanced a civilization that we get, the more being still and meditating is vital to becoming who you need to be in order to achieve your dreams.

Why, you might ask?

Think of it this way. Before a general marches into battle, he studies his opponent. He studies the land.

He studies everything that might come against him when he is ready to move. He doesn't just rush into battle and hope for the best.

And yet, most of our society does exactly the opposite. They see their dream. They march towards it, and when the chaos comes at them, when their world wars for their attention, instead of standing up for their dream, they give up.

As a kid on Guam, we used to have these horrible super typhoons every single year. I am not talking about a little rain and some wind. I am talking about the type of storm that picks up a shipping container and wraps it around a telephone pole "kinda bad," and that's not some made up example. I was amazed when I saw it myself.

The crazy thing about typhoons or hurricanes is they are known for having this moment of utter peace. Where the winds die down. The rain ceases. Everything is eerily calm. It's what meteorologists call the "eye of the storm."

In fact, when meteorologists are watching a storm, they do not watch for the winds. They do not watch for the rain. They watch for the formation of the eye.

They watch for the calm center of a storm starting to form. That tells them that they have an unstoppable, powerful force that is moving in their direction.

Here's the crazy thing. Although the eye is the calmest part of a typhoon. The most powerful part is what meteorologists call the "eyewall." It is the winds that are surrounding that eye that are the most violent, the most destructive, the most damaging.

As a Dreamcatcher, you are that unstoppable, powerful force that is moving in the direction of your dreams. You are the one that has the strength to wrap a shipping container around a telephone pole. You are that undeniable power that is willing to stop at nothing to achieve your dreams.

That's you. And your "eye" is the moment of stillness, of quietness, of preparation.
For a Dreamcatcher, your "eye of the storm" is that time of mediation.

But I get it.

Growing up, I used to think that mediating, silencing the mind, and taking the time to be present, was just for Yoda and anyone of his apprentices that wanted to overthrow the Empire.

Heck, as a kid, trying to tell me to be quiet and peaceful was like pulling teeth. I was a hyperactive kid. But the older I get, the more I realize its importance.

Have you ever watched any of those 'Our Planet' episodes?

I am a huge fan. They are some of my favorites. I especially love watching the ones that follow the lives of some of the most powerful predators that exist today.

If you're ever watching these shows, they'll always choose to follow a beautiful lion or lioness as they roam the safari for their next meal.

The next time you see the option to watch an episode or the next time it is airing, I want you to stop and watch these beautiful animals before they catch their dinner.

Oftentimes, they are just roaming. Out for an evening stroll. Taking a nice little walk. Going about their business.

And then they spot it. They see their opportunity. They know what's on the menu, and they begin to make the move.

At first, these majestic beings seem to just walk in the direction of their prey, but as they get closer to their meal, these gorgeous animals start to get lower to the ground. They find the brush that they can hide in or the rock they can sneak behind. The hunt is on.

But it does not matter what the scenario is. The one thing that these beautiful beasts do, almost every time, is they stop right in the midst of catching their dinner.

They pause. They take a moment to be still.

They could be right in the middle of a stampede, or there could be a windstorm rushing in, or there could be any number of distractions surrounding these 'Kings and Queens of the Jungle,' and in that exact moment, these amazing cats stop before they complete their mission.

As a Dreamcatcher, this is part of rinsing out your glass. You must choose to do the same.

I am not asking that you shave your head. Buy a one-way ticket to the mountains of China and live out the rest of your life in complete and utter silence.

No. Rather, I am saying that in order to catch your dreams, in the chaos that is our ever-moving society, you must stop. You must be still. You must center yourself.

And once you have, game on. You move from there.

Hey, and I get it. If you just can't remove baby Yoda from your idea of mediating, then call it something else.

Call it a moment of silence.
Call it prayer.
Call it being still.
Call it whatever wets your whistle.

But it is a necessity.

So why meditating?

Here's the thing. Meditating, being still, being silent, praying, or whatever else you want to call it is more than just preparing for battle, finding your next meal, or catching your dream.

Meditating actually is a place that not only calms the mind from all the noise both externally and internally, but it also releases you as a Dreamcatcher from the stress of what our lives bring. It brings a center and peace to our world.

It is remarkable to see what happens when we silence the mind for a moment. Not only does it bring a peace into your world, but you will actually find that oftentimes during your moments of stillness, you will

85

receive little deposits, ideas, nudges, inspirations that will come to you in those moments of stillness.

They might be the direction that you need to go in, or your next move, or an answer to a problem that you have not been able to solve. All because you took a moment to rinse out your glass, be still, and meditate.

Don't just take my word for it. Go and try it and watch the benefit that it brings into your world.

So then, how do we find your 'eye of the storm?'

Here are four ways for you to be still and meditate:

    A. Light a candle and just simply focus on the flame. Nothing else. Take 5 minutes and just be still.

    B. Put on soothing music. Close your eyes and just focus on your breathing. 4 seconds in and 4 seconds out.

    C. Take a walk outdoors. Find a place that is away from the hustle and bustle of our world, and just take a walk. Get into nature. No phone. No distractions. Just get outside and enjoy the sun.

    D. Throw on YouTube, and search for guided meditations. There's all kinds of different ones. There are guided ones on calmness, mindfulness, gratitude, focus, clarity, creativity, and the list goes on, and they are for all different types of times, so you pick what works for you.

6. Start Filling Up Your Cup:

The whole point of rinsing out your glass is so that you have a place to pour from. A renewed supply of fresh water that you can give to yourself, to your dream, and give to others.

So…

Fill up your cup.

And what does that look like?

Well, to be honest, it looks a little different for everyone.

If I were to ask you, what makes you smile? What makes you light up? What do you really enjoy doing? Where do you find you lose hours of time? Where do you get the most joy out of life?

What would be your answer?

I asked one of my coaching clients that question as we were working on filling up his cup, and the place that he felt the most joy, the place that lit him up, was on the mat practicing Jiu-Jitsu.

So then, to ensure that we were filling up his cup, Jiu-Jitsu had to be on the menu. It had to be something that he did regularly, weekly, as often as he could.

So, what fills up your cup?

Is it listening to music?
Is it hitting the gym?
Is it going for a run?
Is it getting out into nature?
Is it trying new foods?
Is it traveling?
Is it playing games?
Is it watching movies?
Is it streaming motivational YouTube videos?

Whatever it is, find time in your week, preferably in your day, to fill up your cup. It does not have to be all day. It does not have to be for hours. It literally can be for a couple of minutes.

But find the time to do it. Whatever it is.

So now that you are rinsing out your glass, where do you go to start to move closer to your dreams???

The Art of Dreamcatching

7

The 'F' Words that Everyone Wants to RUN From - Fears, Failures, & F$@K Ups

One of the greatest gifts we have been given on this round spinny thing, floating in outer space, is the gift of fear and the gift of our failures.

I know. I know. I know exactly what you are saying to me right now.

"What the heck does fear have to do with catching your dreams and turning them into reality?"

"And how do failures help me get closer to my dreams?"

You're not going to read many books that tell you the art of catching your dreams, the art of Dreamcatching, the art of turning those dreams into reality requires that you use the gift of fear and that you embrace failure to help you get to your dreams.

Well, I am.

You see fear and failure are like the oil light turning on in your car or the pressure gauge telling you that you are low on air with your tires.

When those things kick on, you don't freak out and run away from the car, screaming at the top of your lungs that you "knew it. You should have never attempted to drive your car. This is a sign. You're walking for the rest of your life."

Nope. That would be stupid.

And if you did try to do that, I'd confiscate your keys and wouldn't let you drive, anyways.

No, the truth is when those 'warning' lights go on, your senses heighten. You are more alert. You watch for every pothole, and you take your car into the service station to get it serviced.

Fear and failure are the same things. They are the warning lights on your dreams that are telling you it's time to get alert and focused. It's time to try a different approach. It's time to seek advice and coaching.

It's time to get into the shop and get things looked at.

I love traveling. It is one of my favorite things to do. I think I love it so much because I have a childhood attachment to it. I also love it because I love getting the opportunity to experience something fresh and new.

But with that said, I hate flying. Probably because I flew over the Pacific Ocean every summer and watched old Superman TV shows where he caught the airplane midair as its nose plummeted. As a child, I realized that if that happened in real life, there'd be no Superman to catch us.

I probably also don't enjoy flying because for 4 years, travel is all I did for work, and I can tell you, flying through thunderstorms, dropping 20 feet as we flew over 4 different tornados, makes one not enjoy flying as much.

And lastly, to rest my case and close this door, I have had my flight rerouted, delayed, lost baggage, canceled enough times that flying isn't my thing unless you're sitting first class or in your private jet.

So why do I share my hatred?

Well, because when it comes to vacationing, especially when traveling in the United States, I would more prefer to jump into a car and drive than to rush to the airport, clear security, and sit at a terminal for however long before they pile us into seats A through Z.

This particular outing, though, I made the ridiculous decision to drive from Seattle down to New Orleans and back. I say ridiculous because, well, it was, and you'll soon understand shortly.

The trip to New Orleans from Seattle is roughly a 39-hour one-way trip. Close to 2,576 miles of road, and depending on how you take the journey, it's across 7 states.

Calculating all of this and not wanting to jump on an airplane, I made sure to have the car fully inspected. Oil was replaced. New tires were added on. The engine was checked, and gas was filled up. This was going to be the trip of a lifetime, and oh was it.

Somehow in my mind, I envisioned crossing the rolling plains, climbing the Rockies, chasing the tumbleweeds. I was expecting to jam out to our favorite tunes, discover small 'hole in the wall' diners that no one knew about, all while making special unforgettable memories as we rode into the creole mecca that is New Orleans.

Instead, a flash flood hit while we were driving through the Rockies. It was so bad that we couldn't see the road in front of us. As far as jamming out to our favorite tunes, we lost cell reception halfway through the trip, and out of pure boredom, I started telling fictional historical facts to those who were naive enough to believe me. I was so excited to get to New Orleans that I made the stupid decision to drive all 39 hrs. straight, so we didn't stop at any cute hole-in-the-wall diners. Nope, if we weren't chugging energy drinks to keep us awake, we were stopping at truck stops so I could get 30 minutes of shut-eye, and then we were jumping back onto the road.

But the funny thing is that isn't even the worse part.

Don't get me wrong. We had an amazing time in New Orleans. I mean a blast. Did a brief pitstop in GulfPort, Mississippi, and since we were in the area, we decided we would make our way through Nashville to visit family.

All seemed well and good until the morning we were meant to depart Nashville and begin the long journey back to Seattle.

As I loaded up the car and kissed the family goodbye, I did a walk around the car just to check everything was good. To my surprise, I discovered that one of our new tires on the front driver side was not only low on tread but was beginning to split and was showing wire.

Now I am no mechanic, but I can tell you that your tires aren't supposed to look like that. And normally, that would be a great sign to take it to the tire shop and replace the tires. But I was on a strict deadline to get back to Seattle, so I rolled the dice and hoped for the best.

Here's what you need to know, and guys, I wouldn't recommend this as great advice, but not only did I decide to drive the 39-hour, 2,576 mile, 7 state, one way trip back on a stripping tire, but I also made the judgment call to not tell my girl what I had discovered.

Now, before you climb down my throat, first I want you to know that I know it wasn't the best decision. Second, in my defense, my girl's nerves don't do well on road trips, let alone road trips where a tire could blow at any moment.

It all seemed fine. The tire seemed to be holding up, and about halfway through the trip, I was sure that we were going to make it back to Seattle with no issues. But it was when we pulled into a small-town gas station in the middle of nowhere Montana that I knew we had a problem.

The small split in the tire that I had discovered in Nashville was now a massive gap and vein. Wires were poking out of the tire everywhere, and to make matters worse, I must not have been able to hold a good poker face because my girl noticed me inspecting the tires, asked me what was wrong, and then discovered to my reluctance the quickly deteriorating tire.

The rest of that trip was a blur. I am happy to say we made it back in one piece. The tire never blew, and first thing Monday morning, I got that bad boy replaced.

But why do I share that story with you?

Because as I drove those 39 long, long, long hours back to Seattle, I was scared shitless. I knew that at any moment, our tire was going to blow. I knew that one pothole was having us call roadside assistance. I knew that we were going to be stranded in the middle of nowhere with no cell reception, and I am no film buff, but if you know anything about horror movies, isn't that always how they start?

And yet, we still made it home.
Was it peaceful?

Not at all.
Were we anxious?

Absolutely. But I want you to understand something, because of our fear, because we were afraid that we were on a one-way ticket to '*The Hills Have Eyes*,' we drove our car like a bunch of granny drivers going for a midday Sunday afternoon cruise around the block.

We were alert. Our eyes were constantly scanning the road for potholes, debris, wild animals, crazy drivers. We drove in the slow lane. We indicated for everything. We drove the speed limit exactly or just under, and we were prepared. We were prepared for anything and everything.

Instead of getting distracted on our phones or by the sights around us, we were hyper-focused on our destination. We had to get there, and we weren't going to allow anything to stop us.

Our fear helped us be better drivers, better than any driving instructor ever could have. I am pretty sure I had my hands 10 and 2 the whole way.

Our fear had us feel every bump. Our fear helped us drive more cautiously. Our fear had us inspect every awkward sound. Our fear helped us be focused on the task at hand. Our fear helped us to be alert.

Fear and Failure...

Actually…

Fear and Failure and your past F$@k ups are amazing teachers of the Art of Perspective. You can look at them as a bad thing. You can look at them as something to avoid and run from. You can look at them as 'why me' 'why can't I ever get it right?'

Or you can choose to look at Fear, Failure, and your past F$@k ups as some of the best teachers, mentors, and coaches there ever was. Fear and Failure are literally teaching you what NOT to do. They are helping you stay motivated. They are helping you stay alert. They are helping you learn from your past mistakes.

I love watching Tom Brady. I especially love watching him play football when everything is going wrong. I especially love watching him play when not only is everything going wrong, but everything is going wrong because it's his fault. But Tom Brady is one of the greats. He is a Dreamcatcher. There is no way he'd have 7x Super Bowl rings if he wasn't.

But the reason I love watching him when everything is going wrong is because he immediately starts to study his failures and his f$@k ups. He embraces his fear. You'll check him watching a film on the sideline immediately after he has thrown an interception, and the thing that is crazy about Tom Brady is that he could have been playing horrible all 3 quarters of the game, but when it hits the 4th quarter, he takes everything that he has learned from his fear, from his failure, from his f$@k ups, and he immediately applies it to helping him comeback and win the game.

It's all a matter of perspective...

***

And this is where the book stopped and sat on the shelf for close to 6 months.

Why?

Because if I was going to be completely honest with you, I was pissed off. I was angry. I was frustrated. I was irritated. I was annoyed. I was disappointed. I was hurt. I was depressed. I felt like a fraud writing a book on catching your dreams when suddenly out of nowhere.

2020 hit.

Yep, I said that right. I started my second book at the beginning of the year in 2020. My hopes were high. My dreams were aspirations. I was excited for what was to come.

And then, out of nowhere, 2020 hit me blindside. And it kept coming. One more thing after another. And for several months, I powered through things. I kept my head on my shoulders. I was proud of the progress that I was making. But as the months longed on, even though my family was doing well, even though our business was booming, even though truthfully things were better than they had ever been before, I couldn't see the light at the end of the tunnel. I wanted to give up, shrink into a little ball, and cry myself to sleep.

Would I never be able to visit my favorite restaurant again?

Would I be confined to virtual 'hangouts' that were nothing like going out and having a good time with my friends?

Would I never be able to travel again?

Would the world shrink to a state of fear, madness, and chaos?

It felt like the world was burning around me. Good friends stopped talking to me out of the blue. Places I had visited before in the past now looked like ghost towns, with the windows boarded up and the doors locked.

And so '*The Art of Dreamcatching*' sat on the shelf, unfinished, because I did not feel like I was in the right space to speak on 'Fear and Failures' when 2020 was hitting me so hard, and I was not rising above it.

And yet, I picked the book back up and began to type again.

Why?

Because too often, we place ourselves in this artificial timeline of when, where, and by what timeframe our dreams have to be accomplished.

And if you don't do that, I know I do, so I'll take the heat for both of us.

But the truth is, who told you that your dream has to happen within a certain timeframe? Who sold you the lie that your dream goes exactly as you planned?

Your dream needs no schedule.

I was at the gym today working out on the elliptical, and generally, I track everything. I track the number of strides I take. I track the distance that I have gone. I track the calories that I have burned. I track the structure of my workouts and the intensity of them.

But I jumped on the wrong machine today. I jumped on the elliptical that didn't care how I liked to track things and challenge myself. I jumped on the machine that had a mind of its own.

My run started out normal. Things were going great, and then out of nowhere, right at the 7-minute mark, my machine turned off, reset all my stats, and then turned back on. Generally, this wouldn't be a problem. I would have just jumped over to a new machine and continued on with my workout, but today all the ellipticals were taken, and I was stuck with the short end of the stick.

So, I turned the machine back on and started working out again. My memory is pretty sharp, and I had an idea of the stats of my 7-minute run, so I would just add it onto my workout at the end. All was good. No problem.

And then, out of nowhere, right at the 7-minute mark, my machine did it all over it again. It turned off. It reset my stats, and it restarted.

At that moment, I had a choice.

Do I get off of my elliptical and call it a quits?

Do I give up and throw in the towel and come back at it again another day?

Or do I suck it up, realize I have the only machine in the entire gym that wants to throw in the towel at the 7-minute mark, power through the resets, the no stats, and continue running until I hit my 40-minute running mark, and then get off this demon child of an elliptical?

I had to reevaluate why I was at the gym. I wasn't there for my stats. I wasn't there so I could track what I was doing. I was there so that I could get in my exercise, raise my heart rate, and sweat like crazy.

My stats didn't matter.

And so, I powered through.

And you want to know the crazy thing?

When I powered through, the machine seemed to realize that I didn't care if it messed with my numbers. I was still going to get my workout in, no matter the cost, whatever it took, and the machine, for whatever reason, stopped resetting at the 7-minute mark and let me power through the rest of my workout.

Sure, I wasn't able to track my stats. And sure, I would have loved to know my numbers, but it wasn't about that. I wasn't there at the gym for that reason.

So WHY do I share this with you?

Because 2020 was a bitch.
I said it. It's out there. No, take-backs.

She wasn't what I expected. I am sure she wasn't what most of us expected, and sure I can cry over spilled milk and talk about all the things I wasn't able to do in the year 2020, or I can remember why I am doing what I am doing. I can study 2020 for what it was, learn from it, pivot and adjust from what I learned, and get on my way.

There are going to be a lot of people that look at the year 2020 and label it as the BIGGEST year of failure they have ever had. They are going to be afraid and fearful because of what 2020 showed them and will not want to move again because of that fear.

But like I said at the beginning of this chapter, before the pandemic hit and before the global lockdowns, and before all the craziness that was 2020, fear and failure aren't something to run from or avoid.

They are your best tools, your greatest assets. They are some of your best allies, even if they sting a little.

Now, you have a choice.

Either you can learn from your fears, from your failures, from your f$@k ups, or you can run from them. Either way, there is no avoiding them. There is no outrunning them. There is no escaping them, and 2020 proved that.

So, my advice would be to learn from them and discover the art of the bounce back.

8

2020 Is Going to Happen. The Global Quarantine Is Coming. Whatcha Going to Do Now?

I think we have established as a kid, I was a rambunctious little one, to say the least. If we haven't, then let me help you understand. I once climbed a telephone pole so that I could get to the top and then let go, trust falling all the way down because one of my friends told me that they would catch me.

Spoiler alert: They didn't.

I have had two concussions, broken my wrist twice, shattered my elbow, shattered my ankle, shattered my heel. I have a permanent road rage burn on my forearm from coming off of a dirt bike. I have cut my knee open twice, playing two different sports. I have dislocated both of my shoulders.

Oh! And I have also torn my hamstring.

What can you say? <u>I love life</u>. I have a lot of energy, and I live life to the fullest.

And this little moment in time will prove no different. Remember, I grew up on a little island. My friend's circle wasn't the biggest, and there weren't many kids my age that lived around me and my family, so I often reverted back to convincing my sisters that they wanted to play whatever absurd game that I had concocted in my head.

Little fun fact. It often worked.

On this particular day, it was no different. I had talked my sisters into playing baseball with me.

Fair enough. Baseball.
How is that too absurd, you ask?

Man! You ask all the <u>right</u> questions at the <u>right</u> time.

Normally, a normal baseball game wouldn't be absurd at all. Nice little game of catch. Maybe break out the bat and hit a few balls. Run around the bases, and slide into home plate.

Normal.

109

But that's not how I do things. That's not how I play. I decided that instead of playing a nice calm game of baseball, we'd up the ante. What if we used a basketball in place of a baseball and played Basket-Baseball? Or Basketball-Base? Or Baseball with a Basketball?

Such a great idea, right!?!

I am sure that it started off well. I know that my sisters and I were having fun, but at some point, the game took a turn. Most likely, what happened was we started taking scores. Then, sure enough, my sisters' score surpassed mine, and it was game on! I couldn't let that happen. Let my little sisters beat me in a game that I created. No way, Jose. Now was my moment to shine.

"Stepping up to the plate, it's number 5, John Bourgeois. The bases are loaded. It's the last inning. The Sisters are up by one. This is it. This is what we have been waiting for, folks. This is what John has been training for year-round. If he doesn't deliver, the Brothers lose the game and have to walk the path of shame the whole way home."

Or at least that's what I remember the 'fake' announcer in my head saying to our non-existent, imaginary stadium full of fans.

110

So, I stepped up to the batter's box. I knew what I had to do. I knew what was resting on the line if I missed this pitch. I had to deliver for all the older brothers around the world. This was my moment.

My sister bounced her pitch.

Hey, like I said, we were playing 'Basket-Baseball.' I had to change the rules somehow.

And when that ball came across the plate, I swung with all my might for the fences.

Now there's a couple of key bits of information that you should know that I left out about this story:

First off, basketballs bounce.

No, duh, Sherlock.

Secondly, the baseball bat that we were using was a wooden baseball bat, and if you're no '*Bill the Science Guy*,' wood transfers energy extremely well. But of course, I am not thinking that when I give it everything I've got. I am thinking about the sound of the fans as I hit a homerun hitter and end the game.

Yeah, none of that happened. My sister bounced the basketball as hard as she could. I swung the wooden baseball bat as hard as I could, and then ball met bat.

And then bat bounced right off of ball, and then the bat came back with the same amount of force that I had given it to clear the basketball over the fences and hit me square in the eye.

Oh, man, did that hurt! I had the worst black eye ever. Needless to say, we never played Basket-Baseball again.

Now I know you are asking yourself, *"why in the world are you sharing this with me, John?"*

Well, besides the fact of wanting to show you how crazy of a kid I was, I want to use this story to chat with you about what you have to do as a Dreamcatcher after you have encountered failures, fears, and setbacks. I want to share with you what you do after you have had a 2020 pandemic, or a global crisis, or a quarantine lockdown sort of setback that hits you right in the eye socket and gives you a nice big shiner.

What do you do then?

You see, every dreamer, whether they are a Daydreamer, a Dreamchaser, or a Dreamcatcher, every dreamer is going to have those moments. So, if you are going to have them, then what should you do after they have come, in order to get back to catching your dreams?

You wanna know what most people do with those moments? You wanna know what Dreamchasers and Daydreamers do with their fears and their shortcomings?

They bury them.
They run from them.
They hide from them.

But that's not you. That's not why you are reading this book. If you're going to be a Dreamcatcher, then none of that can be you. So, what do you do when you get knocked square on your ass and are lying face down in the dirt?

Well, you have to learn The Art of The Bounce Back.

But before I can teach you the Art of The Bounce Back, I must first teach you another art that goes hand and hand with bouncing back. I must teach you an artform that will help you let go of the bruises and cuts that come with your failure. I must teach you an art that

113

releases your setbacks and your shortcomings and sets you up for your dreams.

Why might you ask?

Because if you are a dreamer, which I know you are. If you are a visionary. If you are someone who wants more for your life and knows it's out there, chances are this isn't your first attempt at your dreams. This isn't your first rodeo. I am going to go out on a limb here and say if it isn't your first attempt, that you probably can vividly remember every time you have come short of the prize, every time you have not achieved, every time you have not hit the mark.

And if I can be honest with you, if you are holding yourself to those failures, I can bet, and I am not a betting man, I can bet that you are holding onto the failures of others as well. You are holding onto where they let you down. You are holding onto the times that you needed them, and they didn't show up. You are holding onto the times that they broke you so bad you never thought you would be able to recover.

If that sounds even remotely like you, before I can teach you what it takes to bounce back, we have to choose to first let all of that go.

We have to first learn The Art of Forgiveness.

If we don't, it is like an anchor that will not allow you to continue on your journey because it is pulling you back to your past. Once we release that anchor, once we release that past, it is like rocket fuel for you and your dreams. The sky's the limit.

So, we have to embrace The Art of Forgiveness.

I know. I know. I know.

You're still skeptical. You're still saying, *"What does forgiveness have to do with catching my dreams? What are you talking about?"*

Well, think of it this way. If you have been pursuing your dreams for any length of time, just like we talked about in the previous chapter, you have experienced all types of setbacks. Those little setbacks are like little chinks in your armor, and over time, depending on how long you have been at it, how many chinks you have taken, those chinks begin to add up.

They begin to tell you a false narrative. They begin to feed you this lie that you are unable, and without knowing, you begin to stack those failures, and with each new one, you slowly begin to lose more and more confidence in you and in your dreams.

Well, I am here to tell you.

Confidence is a <u>MUST</u> for Dreamcatchers. Without confidence in you and your dreams, you will not be able to accomplish them. Oftentimes, the only thing that is standing in our way between you and your next level is your setbacks that you are still holding onto.

Well, it's time to release them.

So how do we do that?

We do it by releasing ourselves from those failures and putting aside the past and its shortcomings that come along with catching our dreams. We do that by practicing the Art of Forgiveness

The Art of Forgiveness

First, I want you to take out a blank sheet of paper. Heck, I want you to take out as many blank sheets of paper that you need.

I want you to find a quiet place, a safe place, maybe grab a glass of wine, turn the fire on. You want to get the mood right. The key to this exercise is that you want to be somewhere that is private, and you want to find yourself in a comfortable space.

Next, I want you to write your name at the top of the page, almost like you were writing a letter to yourself.

"Dear John,"

Then underneath your name, I want you to write out the following phrase:

"I forgive you for..."

And then I want you to continue to write.

I want you to write out everything that comes to your memory. Every small and minute memory that you need to forgive, write it all out, and continue to write until you have nothing more to forgive.

Now, I will warn you. This will be a snowball effect. The more you write, the more you will remember. I will also warn you that this will be a draining task, but it is a much needed one for you to catch your dreams. If you are anything like me, wine isn't going to be your only companion. I also lit some candles and had a much-needed box of tissues as I did this exercise myself.

For some of you, this might be a very short exercise, and for others, this might be pages and pages of you forgiving yourself.

But here is my ask:

Complete this exercise to the fullest.
Do not start it and then stop it.
You're a Dreamcatcher
And Dreamcatchers don't do that.

117

Here comes the fun part:

Once you have written out everything that you have forgiven yourself for, I want you to find a place where you can safely burn the pages you have just written out. I want you to put a match to your list. And as those pages burn before your eyes, I want you to symbolically burn them from your memory and let them go. They are no more. You do not need to hold onto them anymore.

Next, in learning the Art of Forgiveness, I again want you to find a place where you are comfortable, a quiet place where you will not be bothered. I want you to close your eyes and imagine that you are at a cafe.

Take a couple of deep breaths in and settle into the moment. Then I want you to imagine that the person or the people that have done you wrong sit across the cafe table in front of you. I want you to take their hands in your hands, and I want you to say the following words to them in your mind:

"John (<u>replace their name here instead of John</u>*), I want you to know that what you did hurt me. It hurt me because* <u>(insert the reason that it hurt you here)</u> *I want you to know that it was not right, but I want you to know that I cannot hold onto what you did any longer, and so*

118

I want you to know that I forgive you for (<u>insert here what</u> <u>they did to hurt you.</u>*)"*

And then, once you have said those words in your mind, I want you to release that person or the people that hurt you from the table. I want you to do this for whomever has hurt you, whomever has done you wrong, or whomever has scarred you, or whomever has betrayed you.

Heck! This is a great exercise for you to sit yourself across the table and spend some time forgiving your own self.

Again, I will warn you. This isn't an easy exercise to do, but I promise you, it is a necessary one. Because like I mentioned earlier in this chapter, you cannot truly step into your dreams if a part of you is still holding onto your past.

But now what?
What do you do from here?
How do you keep fighting?
How do you get back up and try again?
How do you keep chasing your dreams if you are in a moment where we have been knocked down?

Well, you have learned one of the ways to get back up and to continue to move towards your dreams, and that's letting go of your past and forgiving those, including yourself, that have hurt you along the way.

But once you have done that, what do you do next?

I want you to think about a basketball, much like the one that I decided to substitute into my game of baseball. When you think of a basketball, you most certainly think of something that bounces.

Have you ever tried bouncing a basketball on the ground as hard as you could just to see how high it would go?

If you have, I am sure you have discovered that the harder you throw the basketball on the ground, the more force that you use, the higher the basketball will soar in the sky. If you use little to no force, the basketball will barely bounce. If you use lots of power and slam it on the concrete, the ball will bounce high into the sky and over your head.

This is the same with you and your dreams.

This is the Art of The Bounce Back.

It starts with understanding that fears and failures are inevitable and that they are not the end, but rather, they are just the beginning. It is all a matter of perspective. It is understanding that if you have gone that far down, then at some point, you must go that far up.

Think of it like a rubber band.

Have you ever played the game where you and your friends try to see who can shoot the rubber band the furthest?

If you haven't, you're most certainly missing out on life.

But if you have, you'll understand that the further back you pull your rubber band, the more it will soar across the room and win the game.

You are that basketball.
You are the rubber band.

And "the Force is in you, Luke."

Hey! I felt like this was a more than appropriate time to use a Star Wars reference here. Excuse me if it wasn't.

All kidding aside. We understand the concept when it comes to basketballs and rubber bands, but when it comes to our own lives and our own dreams, we want to neglect the very same concept. **Oftentimes, we HAVE to go in the complete OPPOSITE direction of our dreams in order for us to SOAR in the direction of our dreams.**

Oftentimes it will appear that we are going nowhere. It will appear like not only are our dreams not succeeding in the way that we want them to succeed, but they are failing on a massive, colossal scale.

Need an example?

Let's take Steve Jobs. We all know him as the co-founder of Apple, the innovative mind that brought us the iPods and iPhones, the visionary behind much of what we see in the music industry today, with the launch of iTunes.

On August 2, 2018, Apple made history by becoming the world's first publicly traded company to achieve a market capitalization of $1 trillion.

That's a trillion dollars with a capital T.

But Steve Jobs, who originally founded Apple in 1977, was fired from the company nine years after creating it. Imagine being the visionary that Steve Jobs was and being let go by the very company you built out of your garage.

He left Apple in 1985. Purchased controlling stake in a 'no name' company by the name of Pixar. I say 'no name' because, at the time, Pixar was struggling. No one knew about the company, and it wasn't doing well. Much of what you know of Pixar, the "Toy Story," the "Monsters Inc," the "Finding Nemo," was conceived from the years after Steve Jobs was fired from Apple. He didn't just stop with Pixar.

No, Jobs also started to build a new computer company called NeXT. And what's amazing is eleven years later, Apple invited Steve Jobs back to the very company he built, and they ended up acquiring NeXT from Jobs. That acquisition is what led to the creation of the successful iMac and the trillion-dollar company that you know today.

<u>That's The Art of The Bounce Back.</u>

Need another?

Well, let's talk about J K Rowling then. We all know J K Rowling as the infamously creative writer who gave us the amazing Harry Potter series, conceived the remarkable screen writings of the Fantastic Beast franchise, and many other amazing works as well. But what many do not know is that her story did not start there.

To start, her parents never received a college education, but J K Rowling always dreamed about being an author. In fact, Rowling wrote her first book at the age of six – a story about a rabbit, called 'Rabbit,' and then at the age of eleven, she wrote her first novel – about seven cursed diamonds and the people who owned them.

What's interesting to note is that Rowling did not publish the first Harry Potter book until she was thirty-two years old.

Graduating college, moving to Portugal, marrying, and then divorcing, J K Rowling found herself a single mother, living in a small apartment flat, with only the idea of Harry Potter in her mind, but she had a dream, and she began to write.

Jobless and living off of government assistance for years, Rowling would visit several different Edinburgh cafés and hunkered down to write what we now know as Harry Potter and the Philosopher's Stone. She would often bring along her daughter, who would sleep in a stroller right next to her while she typed.

But the story does not stop there.

Even when J K Rowling was finished with the first Harry Potter book, she was then rejected not once, not twice, not even three times by publishers. No, J K Rowling was rejected by 12 different publishers, each one trying to convince her that her novel was not worthy of press.

Fast forward some 24 years later, and we now know:

➤ More than 500 million copies of the Harry Potter books have been sold worldwide.

➤ Each Harry Potter book broke sales records set by the previous book starting with *Harry Potter and the Goblet of Fire*. Book 6, *Harry Potter and the Half-Blood Prince*, published on July 16, 2005, sold 6.9 million copies in the first 24 hours.

➤ *Harry Potter and the Deathly Hallows*, book 7 in the series, was published by Scholastic on July 21, 2007, and had an initial print run of 12 million copies. The book sold 8.3 million copies in the first 24 hours.

➤ The entire Harry Potter movie series is the third highest-grossing film franchise of all time, raking in nearly $9.1 billion as of 2019.

➤ J K Rowling became the first self-made billionaire to obtain her wealth from being a published author.

That's The Art of The Bounce Back.

Still, need more convincing?

Okay, then let's talk about Elon Musk. We all know Elon and his mission to Mars. But before SpaceX was SpaceX, and before Tesla was Tesla, and before PayPal was PayPal, who was Elon before all of that.

Well, truthfully, Elon Musk was a little kid who loved his science fiction and was often bullied when he was younger. He grew up in South Africa at a time of war and civil unrest. But the amazing thing is he always had a dream bigger than himself.

His first major success was X.com which later became PayPal. That gave him the launch pad for Tesla and his true passion for space exploration with his company SpaceX.

What many people do not know is that there was a time in the history of Tesla and SpaceX that things looked very grim. Electric cars had already been tried, and electric cars had also already died.

Now, Elon came along and had a new vision. A vision to build not only an electric car but an elite, sexy electric car and to charge for it in the same luxury classes as some of the major sports cars. Everyone called Elon crazy. It could never be done. No one would buy his cars, and if they even considered it, they would definitely never pay top dollar for it.

If one 'crazy' idea wasn't good enough, Elon Musk also decided simultaneously alongside his electric car adventure to tackle space exploration. Elon wanted to commercialize space much like the airline industry had commercialized the air, but there was one main problem that Elon faced. In order to truly commercial space, one had to solve the problem NASA had faced for over 50 years now.

That problem?

Rockets are too expensive, especially when they are only used once. So, Elon decided that he would find a way to build a rocket that could go into space and then return back to the earth to be reused over and over again.

Now, I am no rocket scientist, but I'll tell you this, the rocket scientists called Elon Musk crazy. They said it could never be done. They said it could never happen.

Elon had already proven himself. He had built a remarkable company with PayPal and sold it. He had the track record, and yet the outsiders looking in, told him to stay in his own lane. They told him that electric cars and space travel were not meant for him. So much so that Elon had to take his investment from the sale of PayPal and put it into Tesla and SpaceX to keep both companies afloat when he could not find investors to invest into his dreams.

Tesla was his first to prove all the naysayers wrong. It quickly became the who's who of cars, surpassing all the giants, being featured on rap videos, and showcased by all who drove them. SpaceX, though, did not have the same success.

Instead, unlike Tesla, SpaceX seemed to be proving all the rocket scientists correct. You could not build a rocket that would be able to return back to the earth.

The first rocket failed.
The second rocket failed.
The third rocket failed.

To you and me, that might not seem all that significant, but those rockets that failed weren't cheap, and every time they failed, the SpaceX team had to start all over again. They had to start at ground zero.

Elon was asked later in an interview, *"That third failure in a row, did you think, 'I need to pack this in.'?"*

To which he calmly and confidently responded, *"Never."*

"Why not?"

And Elon simply said, *"I don't ever give up."*

That's The Art of The Bounce Back.

These are all examples of The Art of The Bounce Back, where everything seemed to be going in the wrong direction, but the truth is they were just getting set up and ready for the launch.

Here's the thing nobody wants to talk about when it comes to dreaming about success. When it comes to dreaming, nobody wants to talk about the fact that you are going to have setbacks. You're going to have moments where nothing goes the way you thought it was going to. You're going to have those moments that punch you in the throat and make you drop to the ground, coughing up blood. You need to know that walking into this fight.

The reason why you need to know that is so many Dreamchasers, so many Daydreamers jumped into dreaming and into going after their dreams with rose-colored glasses on, not expecting that. At some point, they're going to hit a wall and land flat on their face.

So, you need to know going into the fight that there is an opponent, there is going to be opposition, and it doesn't mean you're doing something wrong.

See, that's what happens to so many Dreamchasers and to so many Daydreamers. They walk into their dream. They get a setback, and the next thing you know, they think they were doing the wrong thing because of that setback.

That's the opposite way of thinking.

When you step into your dream, when you start working towards making your dream a reality, you have to know that life is going to come at you and say, "I need your admission ticket."

That admission ticket is your dream. That admission ticket is your adversity. That admission ticket is your obstacle.

You have to go through that "admission ticket" and let life know how bad you want it.

That setback, that adversity, that failure, that failing simply means you are on the right track.

You need to take those setbacks, those adversities, those moments, those times that you're not sure what's going on and nothing is going your way, and instead of looking at it as, 'why is this happening to me? What next? I knew this wasn't going to work out.'

You need to start asking better questions.

- Your questions need to be, "what can I learn from this?"
- Your questions need to be, "what can I get out of this?"
- Your questions need to be, "who can I teach this lesson to?"

The most successful Dreamcatchers understand The Art of The Bounce Back. The most successful Dreamcatchers have an ability to hit a wall, to hit a failure, to hit a setback and immediately spin-off of it and keep going forward.

You must learn to do the same.

As you go after your dreams, you have to figure out how to shrink the time that it takes you to go from a failure to a bounce back.

Too many people wallow in the pit of despair because they say to themselves, *"Woes me. I can't believe I wasn't able to get it on the first try."*

You're not most people. You're a Dreamcatcher.

And so, I want to give you some more ways of one looking at failure, some of which we already looked at in our earlier chapter, and I also want to help you with some practical ways to narrow down the time that it takes for you to get back on your feet and start back up again after you have had a setback.

The Art of The Bounce Back

The first thing that I want you to look at when you're looking at a bounce-back is I want you to set a time limit, a length of time, that it takes you to get over your emotions.

Let me clarify. I was having a conversation with a really good friend of mine. They were going through a relationship breakup, and they were in a lot of pain.

Fair enough, any sort of relationship breakup is going to put you into a lot of pain. And one of the pieces of advice that I gave to this person was:

131

"Hey, I want you to feel the emotion of this moment. I want you to get raw. I want you if you need to, to sit on a couch with a bucket of ice cream, watching your favorite movie. I want you sitting in your sweats. I want you to go ahead and take the moment to grieve this. But what I want you to do that's more important than doing that is I want you to set a time limit for how long you're going to feel these emotions, this pain, your grief for this broken relationship."

I continued to explain to my friend,

"What I mean is if you're going to grieve this for a day, then grieve it for a day. If you're going to grieve it for an hour, then grieve it for an hour. If you need a week to grieve it, then grieve it for a week. But once that timer goes off, you need to get up. Change your environment. Change your mental mindset. Change your emotions. Change your feelings. Get back up and remind yourself of the type of person that you are. You are a champion. You are a fighter. You are an overcomer. You are powerful. You rise above anything and everything that comes at you."

"And after you remind yourself of these things, you need to rise back up. Stand. Head held high and go after things again."

I would also recommend besides setting a time limit on how long you feel that failure that you also do what I like to call a Reset.

Oftentimes we can be running, running, running, running, running, running, running, running, with no rest, and we burn out.

And when that happens *(and my recommendation would be even before that happens,)* you need to be okay, taking a reset, taking a rest day.

In those moments where you've hit a failure, or you've hit a setback, or you've hit a roadblock, those are perfect moments for a reset. It's time for you to self-evaluate. It's time to look at what's going on. It's time to mentally check in with where your thoughts are at and where your emotions are at.

I have found some of my greatest breakthroughs when I was failing and failing and failing, and finally decided, "You know what? I need a reset."

I took a day, call it a "mental day," if you want, and I dedicated that day for myself, where I didn't just dance through a field of lazy daisies, but where I actually practically evaluated what was going on.

I read more than I normally do. I meditated more. I listened to more motivational podcasts. I evaluated what was happening. I looked at the "recordings or the tapes" *(another sports analogy for those of you that don't follow sports.)*

I evaluated the things that would show me what I'd been doing up until that point, and I took the time as I was resetting to analyze them.

By doing that reset by recharging, by refilling, by rinsing out your glass in those moments, and putting in fresh new water, you are allowing yourself to bounce back and go even harder.

So, when it comes to The Art of The Bounce Back, I want you to set a time limit to how long you are going to 'feel' your rock bottom moments. Then I want you when the timer is up to reset. Evaluate the failure. Study it. Learn from it. Once you have reset, it's time to stand back up and start going after your dreams again.

You must learn the art of bouncing back from adversity if you are ever to accomplish your dreams. If you cannot learn how to overcome those moments, then you will not see your dreams become a reality.

Will it come easy?

Absolutely not. It is a skill. It is an art form. It's not something that you're going to just pick up immediately, but by being self-aware and knowing that you need to do it, over time, you're going to see yourself get better and better and better.

And you will watch that not only are you bouncing back, but the length of time that it takes for you to bounce back begins to get shorter and shorter and shorter.

Now that we know how to bounce back from setbacks, whether they be internal or external, let's turn a corner and learn the keys to turning your dreams into reality.

9

It All Starts Here

This is where legends get made. This is where the professionals leave the amateurs in their wake. If you are going to ever catch your dreams and turn them into a reality, if you ever are truly going to be a Dreamcatcher, you must learn the Art of Consistency.

Anyone can make a New Year's Resolution. Anyone can dabble with an idea. Anyone can have a dream and start on the journey towards it, but the Dreamcatchers are the ones that consistently go after their dreams even when they no longer '<u>feel</u>' the hype of starting them.

<u>Consistency is where your dreams begin to take form.</u>

Most dreamers already know that, though. I don't care if you're a Daydreamer, a Dreamchaser, or a Dreamcatcher; you know how important consistency is to your dreams. But I am also sure you are aware of how tough consistency can be as well.

It's tough because, more and more, our world wants things instantaneously. Our world wants their online order delivered in two days. They want their food to be made and ready in 30 seconds. They want the gratification instantly from their likes and follows.

In this type of world, consistency then becomes the ugly stepsister.

Consistency is those early morning wakeups when no one else is even stirring. Consistency is going at it over and over again until you get it down. Consistency is going to the gym even after a rough day. Consistency is moving away from the sweets cause it does not fit into the plan.

And there lies the problem for most people. This is where and why consistency isn't sexy. It's not something you can post about and get 100 likes. Consistency does not give you the instant gratification that our world now craves.

One of my mentors, Jim Rohn, said it best, *"People are rewarded publicly with what they practice privately."*

What that means is so many times, we want it now, but that's not where dreams get made. They get made and turned into reality when no one is looking. They are formed and birthed in the shadows and on the edges.

This is where Dreamcatchers live.

This is where Dreamcatchers thrive.

We all want to praise success, and yet very few are willing to put in the necessary work to get to that success.

Take, for instance, this book. Everyone wants to be a writer. Everyone wants to publish a book. Everyone has a book idea. But the truth is many will start the novel, but very few will finish it.

Why?

Because consistency is not easy. As a Dreamcatcher, you have to have the determination to carve out the time to make your dreams a reality. You have to put in the work to see it come to fruition.

For this book, I had to make the decision to sit down and write. I had to do it when sleep felt better. I had to do it when other activities pulled at my attention and when I wanted to maybe go and do something else.

There were times that I did not know what to write. There were times that my creativity was not flowing the way that I would have liked, but I still typed away. I had determined that I was going to write this book and that I was going to put the necessary time into it to make it happen.

This is what consistency is. It's making the determination that no matter what happens, you will make your dreams a reality.

***

No great feat has ever been accomplished without consistent efforts.

In the exploration of the South Pole, there were two explorers who desired to be the very first explorer to discover it, and both of them set out to accomplish their feat at the exact same time. It was truly a head-to-head battle of who could achieve it first.

One of the explorers was extremely gung-ho on getting there first, and his approach on getting there was to go ahead, and on good days, in the good weather and in good conditions, he and his team would go as hard as they possibly could. If that meant 100 to 200 miles at one given time, they would do it.

But on the bad days, the days that the weather wasn't easy to handle or on the days that the conditions were not favorable, or on the days that it was not safe at all, the team would stop their mission and would only put in the minimal effort they desired for the day.

Sometimes that meant no travel. Sometimes that meant five, ten, maybe even fifteen miles of travel. It was all just dependent on how the team felt under those harsh conditions.

Want to know the funny thing about this head-to-head race?

The funny thing is the explorer that discovered the South Pole and discovered it before the gung-ho team did was the explorer and his team that took the 20-mile approach.

Their approach.

No matter what. No matter the weather conditions. No matter whether they felt like doing it or not. No matter whether or not they were weary or tired, whether they had slept well or not slept well, they committed to doing 20 miles every single day.

On the good days when the weather was fantastic, they would stop at that 20-mile mark and conserve their energy. On the days where the weather wasn't favorable, they would push through the conditions to get to their 20 miles.

They were the ones that discovered the South Pole first.

The same is true when it comes to Dreamcatching.

If you are ever going to catch your dreams, it won't be this stop/start motion. You will never be able to catch your dreams if you can't put the consistent effort behind them.

So, the question then lies, "How can you consistently go after your dreams?"

Well, here's what you have to understand about consistency:

It's very <u>easy</u> to do.

Now. I know you're saying to me, "*Oh my goodness, John, you just finished saying how consistency is one of the toughest things to do, and now you are saying it is easy to do. Which is it?*"

Well.
Yes, it is tough, but it is also easy to do.

This is where many confuse a very simple fact. They think Dreamcatchers are the only ones that are consistent, but the truth is we are all consistent.

We all are consistent at something. Whether it gets us one step closer to our dreams or whether it gets us one step further from our dreams. It is still consistency. Consistency is all about where your priorities are.

I get asked it all the time:
"How do I stay consistent?"
"What do I do in order to build consistency?"

Well, truthfully, like I said above, consistency is easy. It's summed up very simply like this:

Show up
Or give up.

It's that simple.

You need to decide today if you are going to be a Dreamcatcher. You have to decide today that no matter what the conditions are, no matter how you feel, no matter what is happening externally around you, you are going to show up.

No matter what.

You have to decide that you are going to put in the effort necessary to accomplish your goal, and you're going to show up.

If you can't make the decision that you are going to simply show up, no matter what your external world looks like, then you might as well give up the dream, give up the goal, give up what you say you're wanting to do because you're not really invested in it.

I know that can be tough to hear, but if you cannot decide that you will show up for your dream, then the truth is, it's not worth holding onto.

That's just me being honest.

You see those that are consistent, those that show up, those that will accomplish their goals and their dreams, they are invested in their dreams. They are invested in their commitments, and you can see that from their actions.

You show me two different people going ahead and sharing the same dream, the same passions, the same goals, and ask me who's going to achieve their dream.

I'm simply going to ask you, "What are their actions?"

Because their actions, consistently done over time, will determine whether or not they succeed or fail.

Consistency is developed by first making the decision and then aligning your actions and your priorities in that direction. That's where consistency starts. It starts by you deciding that you're going to be consistent today. Consistency starts by you making the decision that you're going to show up today.

And then consistency continues when you make the same decision to be consistent tomorrow.

So, you have learned that consistency is tough in our instantaneously gratifying society, yet you have also learned that it is EASY to do as well.

But as a Dreamcatcher, consistency is so much more than that. Consistency is also something that is empowering and freeing to you as a Dreamcatcher.

How, you might ask?

Well, the power of consistency isn't just around completing your dream and seeing your dreams brought into reality. Although consistency will help you accomplish your dreams, there is also a freeing component that comes with being consistent as well.

So, let's talk about it.

Let's talk about the freeing power of consistency.

You see, as a Dreamcatcher, consistency does way more than just ensure you see your dreams to completion.

1. Being consistent also builds this strong, sure, confident fire in you. This type of confidence that you begin to realize that you ACTUALLY can make your dreams a reality. By being consistently consistent and by watching you accomplish your goals and dreams, you start to show yourself what you truly are capable of, and you begin to believe and know that you truly are

145

a Dreamcatcher. You start to watch the 'Superhero' version of yourself arise, and you begin to find confidence in knowing your true self.

You also begin to understand and find a confidence that you can accomplish <u>anything</u> and <u>everything</u>, and you begin to find a strength in knowing that as long as you give the right consistent effort to accomplishing your goal and your dream, you know it can happen for you.

2. Consistency also trains your body, your mind, and your spirit to trust that when you say you are going to do something… you're going to do it.

There's so much POWER in you knowing that. One of the things that consistency does for a Dreamcatcher, one of the things that consistency does to catching your dream, is it gives you this understanding that you know, that if you said you were going to do it, then you're going to do it because <u>you</u> <u>said</u> <u>you</u> <u>were</u> <u>going</u> <u>to</u> <u>do</u> <u>it</u>.

And now your brain and your body begin to understand,

"Oh, if, if John said, he's going to go ahead and write for 20 minutes, it doesn't matter whether his hand cramps up. It doesn't matter whether he's got writer's block. It doesn't matter whether his kids stayed up very late. It doesn't matter. Cause he said, he was going to do it."

And in doing this, in keeping those promises to yourself, you build this trust between you and yourself. This trust that you keep your word to yourself no matter what.

3. Being consistent also sets boundaries for you and those around you and helps you know what to do, when to do it and if an activity will be beneficial for you and your dreams. It provides you with a type of map or game plan for where you are going and what the next steps are.
On one of the interviews that I had on *The Dreamcatcher Show*, I had the opportunity to speak with the founder of the #100DayChallenge. His whole goal in developing this challenge was to do a set of actions and goals every single day for the course of a hundred days and watch the progress that can be accomplished in doing so.

And so, after having him on the show and watching his journey and seeing what he was doing, I made the decision, 'You know what, I'm going to go ahead and do the same challenge he did.'

He had run a mile every single day for a hundred days.

And I said, "Hey, well, I'm already going to the gym, but why not start running a mile every single day? Let's see how that goes."

Now there were many days when running that mile was extremely easy. When I felt like going ahead and jumping out on the track, or jumping on the treadmill, and where my spirit was high. My body was well-rested. I felt great, and I wanted to run that mile.

Then there were those days when my working days were super long, where I had multiple interviews on the podcast, where I had spent the day writing, working on the business, connecting, networking, investing, and where running that mile felt like such a chore and such a drag in my day. Those were the days where everything in me was fighting and kicking and screaming and telling me that I didn't need to do it.

Here's the thing though, when I started the challenge, I committed to myself that I would be consistent for those hundred days, and in doing so, I created a map for myself.

So, when I got to the period where it was not easy, where it was tough, where I didn't feel like doing it, where my body was aching, and where I was hurting, and where I didn't want to show up, I still did it because I had made the decision way before I began, that I would show up every single day.

And the comical thing is because I made the decision that I would show up every single day, and because my actions aligned with me showing up every single day, the people in my world would get annoyed when they would hear me say:

"Hey, I've got to go to the gym."
"Hey, I've got to go and run my mile."
"Hey, I've got to go on the track."

But they understood that it didn't matter what they said to me; there was nothing that would convince me otherwise not to do it.

There is a freeing, empowering, releasing component that comes with being consistent.

Consistency is not something that you just do when you feel like doing it. There will be many times when you have to be consistent, when you have to put in the effort, when you have to put in the actions, and you flat out don't feel like doing them at all. But if you decide before you begin that you are going to put in the effort, that you are going to put in the actions, that you're going to do whatever it takes to get you closer to your dream and help you move towards your goal, if you decide that you're going to be consistent through it all, then when the going gets tough, then when you don't feel like it, then when you're tired, when you don't want to wake up, when you don't want to call one more client, when you don't want to have one more conversation, then at that point, you've already settled the score with your future self, because you already told your future self, "I'm doing this. Whether or not you want to do it. I'm doing it no matter what."

As you do that over time and you have more and more of those moments where you say, "Hey, I'm doing this no matter what. I promised that I would show up every single day, and I'm going to do it."

As you do that, that consistency element gets easier and easier because your brain, your body, your spirit realizes, "well, there's nothing that we're going to be able to do to convince him otherwise. Might as well just go along for the journey."

Make the commitment today that you are going to be consistent every single day until you've reached your dream.

Make the commitment to yourself today that it doesn't matter what the weather conditions are, doesn't matter what the wind speed is, doesn't matter what the snowfall looks like, you're going to make your dream a reality... no matter what.

Make the commitment to yourself today that you're going to give your dreams the 20-mile approach.

You make that commitment today.

And I promise you, you will accomplish your dream and your goal because you've put the consistent effort behind it.

The Art of Dreamcatching

10

How Do You Eat an Elephant? Well, One Bite At A Time, Of Course!!

We spoke about the importance of consistency in the previous chapter, and we also spoke about how consistency is truly what helped me personally move from being a Daydreamer when it comes to writing, to becoming a Dreamcatcher.

But I want to dive a little deeper into the story (pun intended) of my first book.

You see, yes, consistency was what helped me write "*The Pen and Its Author.*" But that's not where it stopped. Consistency also helped me continue and FINISH The Pen and Its Author.

What do I mean?

Well, let me explain...

When I first started really writing "*The Pen and Its Author,*" the craziest thing happened to me.

I had finally made the decision that I was no longer going to be a Daydreamer and Dreamchaser. I was going to stop just thinking about "writing a book." I was going to stop "having a great idea for a book," and I was actually going to start writing the book and seeing it to completion.

I made the decision to write out the very first edition of "*The Pen and Its Author.*" And when I say I made the decision to write it out, I mean I literally hand-wrote the entire book from front to back before bringing it to print. I wanted to be able to give it to my kids as they grew.

But the craziest thing happened to my very first edition of my handwritten version.

It was stolen.

Yep, that's right.

Stolen, right out of the back of one of my friend's vehicles.

We were out in the city, celebrating my birthday, and my first edition was stolen.

Yep, you read that right. My 'dream' was stolen on the night of my BIRTHDAY.

I had decided to put my backpack in the back of one of my friend's cars. They had parked in a car garage, and it seemed like a great place to park. But someone that night decided they wanted to break in, and they decided to take my backpack from the car. In doing so, my first edition was taken as well.

We searched high and low for that backpack. There was nothing in it of value other than my book, and I just hoped and prayed that the thief would open up the backpack, discover there was nothing in it of value, and chuck the backpack.

But they didn't. And my very first edition was never recovered.

I remember sitting in the coffee shop with a brand-new hardcover notebook with its blank pages. Looking at it, just irritated. I was disgusted with the fact that I now had to start my book all over again.

I had to go ahead and pour my blood, sweat, and tears back into something that I had already started. And then it was stolen from me.

I remember literally thinking to myself, "*Gosh, I don't want to do this. I do not want to pick this book back up. I do not want to go ahead and have to write it all over again. I have already written it. This isn't fair.*"

But I made the decision that I had to get over myself. I had to get over my frustration. I had to get over the fact that it wasn't fair. I had to get over the fact that I wished it hadn't happened. I had to get over the thought of "*Gosh, 'if only' I had gone ahead and put my backpack somewhere else and maybe not carried my book inside my backpack.*"

I had to get over that, and I had to start all over again and begin the process once more.

Now had I not made that decision to pick up and start again, my first book, *"The Pen and Its Author,"* would never have been written.

In fact, this book that you are reading now probably would have never been written had I not made the decision that I was going to get over that hiccup.

> *Was it fair?*
> No.
> *Did I wish it hadn't happened?*
> Yes.
> *Would it have been nice to not have to rewrite the entire book?*
> Absolutely.

But I had to make the decision that I was going to overcome that objection, that I was going to rise above it, and that I was going to keep moving forward.

Now I share that story with you because I want you to understand the power of consistency and how important and necessary it is to your dreams. I also want you to understand how detrimental consistency can be to your dreams as well.

What do I mean?

I mean this. I chose to continue to write even after my book was stolen, but I could have easily made the decision to continue to wallow in self-pity and consistently NOT write the book.

You need to understand if you are consistently doing the wrong things, the things that are taking you in the opposite direction of your dreams, then you are going to find that you are consistently moving further and further away from your dreams. On the flip side, if you are consistently moving one step closer to your dreams, you will find that eventually, you will achieve whatever it is that your heart desires.

So, the real question then becomes, how do you know which direction you should go in, in order to make your dreams a reality?

Well, I would like to present to you, The Decade Approach.

This concept is derived from a speech that I heard Jeff Bezos, the founder of Amazon, give. He was speaking at a keynote about the moment when he decided to quit his job, leave everything he had already built behind, and branch out into the unknown, on a venture that he was unsure he would be successful at.

He said, *"The best way to think about it was to project myself forward to age 80 and say look when I'm 80 years old, I want to minimize the number of regrets that I have. I don't want to be 80 years old in a quiet moment of reflection, thinking back over my life and cataloging a bunch of major regrets. And I think that regrets, our biggest regrets in most cases... turn out to be acts of omission. It's paths not taken, and they haunt us. We wonder what would have happened... And that's the frame of mind that I put myself in. And once I thought about it that way, it was immediately obvious to me. I knew when I am 80, I would never regret trying this thing that I was super excited about and failing. If it failed, fine. I would be very proud of the fact that when I am 80 that I tried, and I also knew that it would always haunt me if I didn't try. And so that would be a regret. It would be a hundred percent chance of a regret if I didn't try and basically a 0% chance of regret if I tried and failed."*

Wow! Catch that. Jeff Bezos fast-forwarded to his 80-year-old version of himself and made the decision, if his 80-year-old self would regret not going for it, then it meant his present version had to go for it.

What an amazing relieving concept.

Imagine being able to know what you needed to do today to help you achieve your dreams of the future while also knowing what you needed to start saying 'no' to so that you could fully start focusing on those dreams.

That's The Decade Approach.

Tony Robbins said it best "most people overestimate what they can do in a year, and they underestimate what they can do in 10 years."

Well, you're not "most" people; that's why you're reading this book, and so we are going to take an exercise that we did earlier in the book and expand on it even further.

The Decade Approach:

You already spent the time working on a "...Year From Now." Now I want you to expand that vision, but before we can do that, I first want you to start by asking the following question:

1. Where are you?
Where are you currently in comparison to your dreams?
Be honest with yourself.

Are you broke?
Are you unorganized?
Are you a people pleaser?
Where are you?

The reason it is important to know where you are is because it helps you understand what hurdles you might have to overcome, what type of people or processes you might have to put in place to get you to your dreams, and frankly, even what sort of things you need to start saying no to.

If you're an aspiring Olympic athlete, and you aspire to win the gold, then staying up late, Netflixing, and eating a whole bag of Lays Ketchup Chips is something you're going to have to start saying no to.

So, take the time right now, and write out where you are. Divide it into sections.

Where are you mentally?
Where are you physically?
Where are you financially?
Where are you spiritually?
Where are you relationally?

Once you have done that, we can start with the next part of The Decade Approach

2. Where do you want to go?

"Without a vision, people perish." This cannot be more true for you as a Dreamcatcher.

You need to know where you want to go, and similarly to Jeff Bezos' and to Tony Robbins' words, I want you to start thinking bigger.

It's great to imagine and have a vision for a year from now, but where do you want to be in ten?

What do you want to have in the bank?
What do you want to have accomplished?
Who do you want to be hanging with?
Where do you want to be living?

You see, with a decade approach, you can have a year like 2020 and go, "oh, that's only a tenth of my time in a decade, no biggie."

So, I want you to take a moment and write out where you want to be in 10 years.

You'd be surprised what can be birthed in ten years and what can be laid to rest in ten years.

In ten years, Blockbuster was laid to rest, and Netflix was born. In ten years, the purchasing of songs on iTunes shifted to streaming music on platforms like Spotify, YouTube Red, and Apple Music. In ten years, companies like Nikon, Panasonic, and other portable camera companies were replaced as their consumers shifted from their portable cameras over to their cell phone cameras.

Imagine what you can accomplish in ten years as you structure your life around your own Decade Approach.

So, take some time. Put the book down and write out where you want to be in 10 years.

Now that you have created the vision, what do you do next?

Where do we go from here?

Well, the next step is to think about why you want to be there in 10 years.

- What is it about that vision that inspires you?
- Why did you put down that destination versus somewhere else?
- Why is it important for you?

The reason it is crucial that you answer the above questions is because as you begin to work on your dreams, as you begin to transition into being a Dreamcatcher, you will have the times where you must pull on the reason that you started going in that direction, to begin with.

Let your "why" be your anchor as the storms of life come your way.

As a dreamer, I am sure you have heard it before, "you've got to have a strong WHY."

I don't know about you, but I always struggled with figuring out "why" my dreams were so important to me until I came across an amazing exercise from one of my mentors and one of the books I read. *(Dean Grazsoi has been an amazing mentor of mine & the book, not written by Dean, but instead written by Steve Sims was Bluefishing)*

The concept is very simple.
Ask yourself:

"Why are you doing this?"
"Why is it important for you?"
"Why MUST you make your dreams a reality?"

Once you have your answered, Dean calls it the "7 Layers of Why," & the book, "Bluefishing," talks about diving deeper into the why, but whether you do it the 7 Layers Deep method, which is simply taking your answer and asking why 7x more times, or if you decide to do it the Bluefishing way and only ask why 3x more time, either way, by diving deeper, you come to realize what is really driving you, what is really pushing, and what you really want to hold onto when you are working through the tough times.

So, we have tackled having a Decade Approach to your life and your dream. We have tackled discovering why your dream is REALLY important to you, but we still have that lingering question that so many people stop with.

I know the dream.
I know why I want to do it, but HOW?
How do I make my dream a reality?
How do I become a Dreamcatcher?
How do I make it happen?

And this is where I want to introduce to you the Art of the Small Wins.

There are two sayings that I am sure you are very familiar with:

The first was said by Desmond Tutu.
"There is only one way to eat an elephant: a bite at a time."

And the second is an old Chinese proverb by Lao Tzu.

"A journey of a thousand miles begins with a single step."

Both of them ask the same question and then deliver the same answer.

How do you eat an elephant?
One bite at a time.

How do you take the journey of a thousand miles?
One step at a time.

It's the same concept, just expressed in a different way. The way you accomplish any large feat, or dream, or vision is to complete the smaller tasks that make up the larger one.

So how do we apply that reasoning to your vision for your next 10 years?

We do that by breaking down the large dream into slightly smaller dreams and working on those first. And if you find that your 'broken down smaller dreams' are still too large for you, then you break it down again, and again, and again, until you come to something that you are able to accomplish every single day without even batting an eye.

Let me give you an example.

One of my large audacious dreams is that "I am an international New York Times Bestselling Author."

That's the BIG dream, but if all I focus on is that dream, then I get angry and disappointed because I am constantly reminded of the realization that that dream is not accomplished.

So, what do I do?

And what do you have to do when the dream is bigger than your reality?

Well, you have to break it down.

You have to break it down even smaller.

For me, the dream is to be an international New York Times bestselling author. But the realization is I'm not that yet, so what do I have to do?

Break it down to a smaller dream.

Well, if I'm not an international New York Times bestselling author yet, then the smaller dream would be that "I am an author."

But here's where the problem lies. When the big dream came to be a dream of mine, I was not an international New York Times bestselling author. I wasn't an author. I wasn't even published.

So, breaking it down to "I am an author" is still too large of a dream.

So, what did I have to do again?

I had to break down the dream even more.

If I am not an international New York Times bestselling author yet, and if I'm not an author, and if I'm not even published, what can I do?

What can I control today that will bring me closer to my dreams and eventually to my big dream?

Well, in my case, I can control one thing with this dream. I can do this one thing consistently, every day. I can control that "I am a writer."

That I can control. I can show up for that every day. I can do that for a decade.

And when I say, or when I write out, or when I work on my dream that "I am a writer," my mind is in alignment with me. It does not think that I am lying to it or trying to deceive it. It understands that I am.

The same is true about you and your dream.

I don't care if your dream is to have a platinum album.

How do you break that down to something you can control every day?

I don't care if you want to be a famous actor.

How do you break that down to something you can control every single day?

I don't care if you want to be the next Michael Jordan, Elon Musk, Mark Cuban, or Oprah Winfrey.

How do you break that down to something you can do every day and that can align with you when you say it?

167

This is where the power of small wins comes in. This is where Dreamcatchers blow past the competition.

You see, the concept of the art of the small wins is very simple. Like we demonstrated above, first, you have to have your Decade Approach, where you are going. Then you have to know why you are going there and what it means to you. Once you have those, then you take that BIG dream and break it down to something that you can deliver on every day that will get you one small step closer to your large dream.

Here's where the art of the small wins comes in.

What you are doing by working on those micro dreams that make up your larger dream, is that you are creating things that you can easily, and quickly, and consistently achieve on a regular basis. You are creating things that you can control and do while not having to worry or be concerned about outside obstacles or barriers.

You are stacking the deck in your favor. You are giving yourself small goals, small dreams, small aspirations that you know you can achieve.

> They're easy to do.
> Still work on your part.
> Still a stretch.
> But easy to do.
> And totally in your control to complete.

And here's the really cool thing. As you begin to complete these small wins, what happens is you begin to build momentum. You begin to build confidence in yourself and your ability. You begin to realize that if you can catch these smaller dreams, then you MUST be able to catch your larger dreams, and as you begin to catch your larger dreams, you start to realize that your HUGE CRAZY FARFETCHED dream is actually something that is obtainable and something in your wheelhouse that you can do and achieve.

And before you know it, you have created so much momentum and developed so much confidence that you look up and realize that you have achieved your Decade Approach.

You have walked the journey of thousand miles.

You have eaten the entire elephant.

One bite at a bite.

That is how momentum is created.

Much like a snowball rolling down a hill, as you begin collecting small wins, you begin to collect more and more wins along the way, and they start to go faster and faster.

The things that felt like a challenge before don't feel like a challenge anymore. Doors just start swinging open for you. You start meeting exactly the right people at exactly the right time. You begin to build this confidence that you can achieve all of your dreams. Your belief starts to strengthen. Your skillset starts to develop.

That's the power and the art of the small wins.

Now here's a little exercise along the way to help you collect your small wins and will help you start to see the progress you are ACTUALLY making towards your BIG dream.

This exercise is super simple. There isn't much to it, but I want to warn you, it is super powerful on creating momentum around your life.

Please remember anything that is simple, anything that is easy to do is also easy not to do.

To give you a little backstory on this exercise, I started doing it after all hell broke loose in 2020, and I started doing it at the start of 2021 as I was reflecting back on 2020 and was reflecting on both the blessings of the year and on the learnings from the year.

What I came to realize was that I had a remarkable year in 2020, but what I learned was because I was not daily, weekly, and monthly reflecting back on those wins, I was mentally viewing my year as a failure rather than as a success, and so in a way to combat that and in a way to ensure that I see all the small wins along the way, this exercise was birthed.

It's called The Success Calendar.

All you will need for this exercise is a calendar.

I use my phone's calendar, but you can also use a traditional calendar as well.

It's really up to you.

What I want you to do for this exercise is each day label the day as a Success.

Then under that label, I want you to write out everything about the day that made it be a success.

Make sure that you are collecting all of your small wins.

It should look something like this:

Success:
- Woke up at _____
- Meditated
- Journaled
- Read for _____
- Wrote for _____
- Workout
- Ran for _____
- Stayed under my caloric deficit
- Picked my kids up from school
- Kissed my significant other
- Etc.
- Etc.
- Etc.

I think you get the gist, but I want you to make sure that as you are writing out your wins, you are not missing anything.

Make sure that these small wins align with your Decade Approach and align with where you want to be in 10 years.

Next, once you have completed writing out your successes for seven days, I want you to take all the wins from those previous seven days, and I want you to compile them all together under one successful banner for the week.

Successful Week 1 of _____ [insert the year here]:

- Woke up at _____ for _____ days
- Meditated for _____ days
- Journaled for _____ days
- Read for _____
- Wrote for _____
- Workout for _____ days
- Ran for _____
- Stayed under my caloric deficit for _____ days
- Etc.
- Etc.
- Etc.

And what's important here is that you tally up the sum of the last seven days into one final number for the entire week.

Meaning, if you were reading for 10 mins each day, then under this success banner, you want to put, "Read for 70 minutes."

Another perfect example, if you are running a mile each day, then under your success banner, you'll want to put "Ran for 7 miles."

A Little Hint: This is why I like using my phone's calendar because I can just copy and paste each success that I had for the last seven days back into the final week's numbers.

And lastly, you do the same thing for the end of the month and the end of the year.

Successful Month 1 of _____ [insert the year here]

- Woke up at _____ for _____ days
- Meditated for _____ days
- Journaled for _____ days
- Read for _____
- Wrote for _____
- Workout for _____ days
- Ran for _____

- Stayed under my caloric deficit for _____
days
- Etc.
- Etc.
- Etc.

Followed by:

<u>Successful Year</u> _____ [insert the year]
- Woke up at _____ for _____ days
- Meditated for _____ days
- Journaled for _____ days
- Read for _____
- Wrote for _____
- Workout for _____ days
- Ran for _____
- Stayed under my caloric deficit for _____
days
- Etc.
- Etc.
- Etc.

I'll tell you this.

You come back and look at what you have accomplished in a week, and then in a month, and then in a year, and you'll be fired up to keep going because you will start to see how all those small wins that you thought were insignificant, suddenly begin to add up to your "thousand-mile journey."

Secret Hint (this is the pre-workout juice you take right before a gnarly workout session at the gym):

If you start your day and label it a success before you begin, write out all the micro wins that you are going to have for the day, and then come back at the end of the day and verify that you achieved them, not only are you seeing the small wins for the day but you are also setting an intention over your day that hones in your focus for what you need to accomplish

Like I said, it's your NOS to your already 'supped up' engine (hey…who doesn't need a good 'ole Fast N Furious 2000s reference?!? I know I sure do.)

That is the power of small wins. Compounding over and over again.

The Art of Dreamcatching

11

It's Not the Right Time. Actually… It's Now or Never

A while back, I watched the now quite famous YouTube video, "The Time You Have (In JellyBeans)" If you haven't watched it, definitely find some time to crack open your laptop and put it on.

Here I'll even provide you the link so you can go right to it:

(https://www.youtube.com/watch?v=BOksW_NabEk)

But if you haven't seen it, I'll give you a brief overview of the video or for those of us who might need a refresher.

On average, our lives equal roughly 28,835 days, AND in this now viewed by 8.1 million different viewers, YouTube video, the creator of the video counted out 28,835 JellyBeans.

(I want to know if the producer had to go to one candy store for that or 100.)

And with those JellyBeans, he walked us through how most of us spend our 'JellyBeans.'

- *Most of us will be asleep for 8,477 days.*
  - *We will be in the process of eating, drinking, and/or preparing food for 1,635 days*
- *We will be at work for 3,202 days.*
- *We will be commuting and/or traveling for 1,099 days.*
- *On average, we will watch some form of TV, streaming service, or show for a total of 2,676 days.*
- *We will spend 1,576 days on household activities, like chores, tending to the pets, or shopping for the home.*
- *We will care for the needs and wellbeing of others, our friends and family, for a total of 564 days.*
- *We will spend 671 days bathing, grooming, or sitting on the toilet.*
- *We will give 720 days to community activities like religious and civil duties, charities, and taking classes.*

Once we remove all of those days or those JellyBeans, we are left with a total of 2,740 JellyBeans.

That's a grand total of 2,740 days remaining. Some of us will have a few more, and some of us will have a few less, but in essence, we will have roughly a total of 2,740 left over.

So, the question then is, what will you do with that time?

You see, most of us, our daydreamers or our dreamchasers, they will just 'eat' the remainder of those 'jelly beans' and call it a good time.

But I want you to take a moment and really ask yourself, what will you do with that time?

2,740 days. That's not a lot when you boil it down.

We have only been given this gift today.
The present.
Never tomorrow
And never to relive yesterday.

This is where so many dreamers fall off. They conceive the dream. They discover the why. They build the action plan for the small wins that they are going to take, but then they stop.

They stop dead in their tracks, even with all of the momentum that they have created, and this is where many dreams die. They die because of the false pretense that the dreamer will start working on his or her dream when the timing is right. They take a look at their

179

surroundings, and they say to themselves, "I'll start when [xyz] happens."

And this oftentimes is the end of their dream.

It was the death of my dream for the longest time. It's one of the reasons that I would get extremely excited about a new idea, a new dream. I'd go work on making it happen. Would hit my first real obstacle and then would start making excuses as to why I needed to put it off to another time.

I'd make the excuse:

"Oh, when I have enough money, then I'll start."
"When I have 'the' good paying job, then I'll begin."
"When I'm done moving, then that will be a good time to start."
"When my firstborn is born, then things should be slower, and it'll be the perfect time to begin."
"When I have the right investors, then I can really go after things."

And on and on and on, the excuses would go.

If only I could go back in time and have a conversation with my past self, I'd share the same things that I'm going to share with you.

There is no "perfect time" for your dreams.

Sorry to burst that bubble for you.

The perfect timing is but an illusion. It's but a mirage. The closer you get to the "perfect time." The further and further it moves from you.

In fact, every time I'd get close to the 'perfect time,' I'd make a new excuse for when I would start and why I couldn't quite start now. The funny thing is when I actually started, and I mean really started going after my dreams, was when I hit rock bottom. And I mean complete rock bottom.

I had had everything that could be defined as the 'perfect time.' I had the house. I had the car. I had 'the' amazing job. I had the kids. I had all the friends. But I didn't start turning my dreams into a reality until I lost all of that.

You caught that right.

My surroundings lined up with the 'perfect timing,' but I didn't start going after my dreams and turning them into a reality until I lost all of it. I had to go from having it all to having none of it.

I lost the car. I lost the house. I lost the family and the friends. I lost the job and the funds in the bank, and the great credit. I lost it all.

I went from having 'it' all to sleeping on a floor in a 750 square ft apartment. No furniture. No bed. No car. No money. Only getting to see my kids for 8 hrs. on a Saturday.

And it wasn't until I was walking down the aisle at my grandfather's funeral. Faced with how fragile life REALLY is and how at any moment, we can be present, and then we can be gone, that it hit me. I had to start going after my dreams.

It wasn't until I saw my grandfather's tin urn at the end of the chapel that I realized the truth. We never know when our time is up, and if we don't know when the movie ends, then we better start working on the opening scene now.

And I am sorry to be morbid in our discussion of catching one's dreams, but it's so important that you understand this.

Les Brown says it best "The richest place on earth is the graveyard."

182

Their dreams have died with their dreamer.

We don't know how much time we have on this spinning rock, and if we don't know how much time we have, why not use the time that we do have.

I heard it said the other day, "lead when no one is listening." And I am going to take that a little further for us:

Speak when no one's listening.
Act when no one's watching.
Write when no one is reading
Do when no one's doing.

So many times, we allow the roadblocks of life to stop us, and we say to ourselves, "I'll wait. I'll start going after my dream once 'this' *[insert situation]* happens. Then I'll go after it. Then I'll really make it happen."

But that is not the way that you will ever be able to catch your dreams.

If you continue to push off your dream, your destiny, your vision, your goals to this to illusive "when this happens" timeframe:

When I have this much money…
When I've made these connections…

When the kids are off to college...
When I have a baby...
When I don't have a baby...
When I have a job...
When I don't have a job...

If you keep pushing your dreams off to that time period, you will never ever catch your dreams.

Your dream will keep alluding you much like a rainbow. The closer and closer you get to your "perfect scenario," you will discover that there will always be the next situation that arises that you have to say, "Ah, well, actually, once this happens, then I'll go ahead and do it."

You see, I want you to envision your dream as your favorite meal. I mean, your absolute favorite. You know the meal I am talking about.

It's that meal that you always crave, that one, that as you're thinking about it, your mouth begins to salivate. Whenever anybody asks you, "where do you want to go?" That's the meal you think of, and that's the place you always suggest because of it.

It's the meal that when the friends, the family, the loved ones are over, you always make. You know the meal I'm talking about.

Well, I want you to imagine your dream as that meal. They're amazing. They're wonderful. They are delicious. But I want you to think about this. If you were to take your favorite meal, and you were to go ahead and leave it out on the counter.

Don't refrigerate it.
Don't put it away.
Don't Saran Wrap it.
Don't put any foil on it.

Just leave it on the counter.

Or better yet, let's say you took a bite of that meal. Oh, and it tasted so good. But let's say I said to you, "All right, you got to leave your favorite bite in your back jaw, right behind your wisdom teeth. You can't, you can't let it go down. You just gotta keep it there."

Here's what I can promise you. I promise you over time, whether it was on the counter or it was in your mouth, eventually, that meal will begin to sour. That meal will begin to decay. That meal will begin to taste disgusting, and gross and everything that you loved about it, you will now hate.

Why?

Because you did nothing with your favorite meal. You didn't eat it. You didn't put it away. You didn't digest it. You didn't give it away. You didn't let a friend eat it. All you did was allow it to spoil and decay. By doing nothing with your favorite dish, you ruined it and killed it.

Your dream will react the exact same way.

The longer you push it off. The more you push it off. The more you say, "I'll do it later." All you are really doing is allowing your dream to decay.

You are allowing your dream to spoil. Eventually, the thought of your dream will disgust you and will drain you.

I need you to understand something.

I don't care how large your dream is. You need to make the decision to start.

You need to make the decision to start NOW.

You will never catch your dream if you do not start now. You will never see your dreams accomplished unless you start today. Starting now does not mean that your big audacious dream is SUDDENLY accomplished right then and there in the moment.

No.

What it means is that you have begun the journey. You have started to take the necessary steps needed for your dream. You have started to walk your dream out.

I need you to understand me when I say this. Your dream, no matter the size of the dream, your dream will always take the exact same amount of time, whether you start it today, or you start it tomorrow, or you start it ten years from now.

It is always going to be the same length of time in order to see it to completion.

Let's put it this way:

If I were to say to you, I need you to go from Seattle to Los Angeles. Here's what we know. There's an adventure that you will have to partake in order to get from Seattle down to L.A.

The truth is it doesn't matter when you start, how you start, what you do to start. You still will have to make the same journey from Seattle to Los Angeles.

The journey still needs to be had.

If it doesn't happen, you remain in Seattle and never get to see the Hollywood sign, never get to walk the famed stars, never get to jump into the warm Pacific Ocean.

The route does not change depending on your timing. The route remains the same for the destination that you are seeking to obtain. It never changes.

So, if that is the case, wouldn't it be wise? If you're trying to go from Seattle down to L.A, wouldn't it be wise for you to start sooner rather than later?

I mean, the journey is going to still be the same length no matter when you start. I don't care if you are walking, hitchhiking, jumping in the car, jumping on a plane, jumping on a bus, jumping on a train. It doesn't matter. The sooner you start, the sooner you get to your destination.

Starting does not change the length of your journey. It does not shorten it by starting sooner. It does not lengthen it or make it easier by procrastinating and waiting until later. The journey will remain the same when you make the decision to start.

If this is true, if the journey remains the same, then you have to choose to begin today. You have to choose to begin now, to walk out those steps necessary now to get you to your dream.

Understand. Time is an illusion. It's fake. It's not real, and therefore the perfect timing is an illusion as well.

My background has been helping people make decisions, and what I have found is if a person is inclined to state that the timing isn't right, then that person will consistently find a reason why the timing isn't right. They will consistently replace the old reason with a new one.

As humans, we have this myth that we have all the time in the world. That the perfect timing will show up flashing lights, with a marching band, and will announce itself to us.

Here's the problem.

If we keep waiting, one day, you'll wake up and realize your opportunity is long and gone.

Seneca the Younger wrote these words in "On the Shortness of Life" that so greatly describes the dilemma that most Daydreamers and Dreamchasers are in:

"You live as if you were destined to live forever, no thought of your frailty ever enters your head, of how much time has already gone by, you take no heed. You squander time as if you drew from a full and abundant supply, though all the while that day which you bestow in some person or thing is perhaps your last."

Now I don't want this to be some somber message for you, but I do want you to understand the lesson I had to ask myself as I was staring at my Papo's silver tin and as I looked at the photo of my grandfather that I had known so well.

"How much time do I really have to make my dreams a reality?"

Like, take a moment. Right now, take a moment, and ask yourself, "If a doctor told me today that I had a week to live, or a month to live or 6 months to live or a year to live, what would I do with my remaining time?"

Now I am not saying up and quit your job, grow the beard out, and run across the states like Forest Gump did, but I am wanting to introduce to you something that is absolutely a MUST when it comes to catching your dreams.

And that is the power of Now.

Have you ever asked yourself why people wait to pursue their dreams? Like really asked yourself, what stops most people from going after it?

The truth is they do it for three main reasons:

Fear. Distractions. And the elusive idea of the Perfect Timing.

So, if those are the three main reasons that Daydreamers and Dreamchasers never pursue their dreams, what do you need to do to be a Dreamcatcher and catch your dreams?

You need to:

1. Embrace Your Fear
2. Eliminate Your Distractions
3. Empower Your Now

Embrace Your Fear

Fear stops most people because they are afraid of the unknown, and they are more comfortable with their known.

Knowing that.

How do you embrace your fear and step into the unknown, the place where dreams become reality?

Well. Like we chatted about earlier in the book, the first step is to change our perspective on fear. You have to move from running from your fears to embracing them and seeing them as a guide and a teacher.

But the truth is we have all been there. We have all had those fears creep up on us.

Those moments when you are on the top of the roller coaster. Everything has stopped. The ride is rocking back and forth, swaying in the wind. You can hear the creaking of the carts, your hair begins to stand, and fear takes over.

So, what can you do in those moments to help you embrace your fear?

1. <u>Breathe deeply</u>. I mean it. Fill those lungs up with air and bring yourself into the moment. Breathing deeply lowers your blood pressure, slows your heart rate, and sends 'feel-good hormones,' like serotonin and oxytocin, to the body,

2. <u>Change your perspective</u>. View the fear from a place where your dreams have already been accomplished, and you are looking back on them now and seeing how ridiculous they actually were.

3. <u>Take a moment</u> to think about all the beautiful, all the incredible things in your life that you are thankful for, grateful for, and are TRULY miracles in your life. *(You know... like I don't know... the fact that you just took another breath without having to think about it, the fact that your heart just pumped life through your entire body, the fact that this spinning rock, we call Earth, doesn't just spin you off of it and send you hurtling through space... Find those things and reflect on them)*

In those moments, instead of doing what most do, embrace your fear and understand by doing so, you are coming one step closer to your dreams. Put your hands in the air, scream at the top of your lungs, and enjoy the ride.

Eliminate Your Distractions

Is this helping me get one step closer to my dream?

Or is this taking me away from it?

You want to know what stops so many people from getting up and actually working on their dreams, from actually taking action now and making their dreams a reality?

It is the distractions that they allow themselves to get distracted by.

It's too easy. Distractions are everywhere.

We live in a world that is constantly vying for our attention, constantly shouting at us to look here, go there, buy this, avoid that, consume these, stay away from those.

And because of that, we, as Dreamcatchers, have to be intentionally intentional. If we really want our dreams to manifest themselves, we have to ask ourselves, "Is this helping me get closer to my dream, or is it distracting me from it?"

As a Dreamcatcher, you have to be hyper-aware of where your focus is, and as a Dreamcatcher, you have to be mindful of how you use your time and where you put your efforts.

<u>You must be intentionally intentional.</u>

You might read that and not grasp the truth.

So let me phrase it this way.

If you are seeking to be a Dreamcatcher and want to make a new life for yourself, here's what I would challenge you. Hold onto being intentional and start to apply it to your day-to-day life. You'll quickly discover its truth.

What I have learned as I have studied other Dreamcatchers and what I have found has drastically transformed my own life, and my own world is this:

You have to be <u>intentionally intentional</u> about everything:

Your time.

Your tasks.

Your relationships.

Your words.

Your thoughts.

What you watch.

Who you follow.

Who you listen to.

The level of effort you put into your tasks.

You see, most of this world moseying around like catfish in a swampy Mississippi river. Bumping into the world around them and taking whatever is given to them. And then, from their catfish bumpy, daydreaming mindset, they complain about how it's not fair and how they wish it was a different way. The problem is they have had the steering wheel the entire time but have chosen not to drive.

If you want the life you've always dreamed of, decide to be intentionally intentional. Grab the steering wheel, eliminate the day-to-day distractions, and steer yourself in the directions of where you want to go.

If you are not sure whether or not something is a distraction or a step in the right direction:

Then ask yourself.

Is this helping me get closer to my dreams?

If it's not, then eliminate it.

Now… you wanna take it even one step further?

Wanna put some NOS into your dreams like they did in those cars from Fast and the Furious 1, 2, 3,… 9?

- Turn off the TV, The Netflix, The Stream
- Stop Watching The NEWS
- Quit Scrolling the Feed
- Eliminate the excess noise (That's your own voice of fear. That is the voice of

fear from others. That is the voice that flat out isn't helping, but it is just straight up hindering you.)

And then, from there, not only will you find that you are focused, but you'll also find you have the ability to empower yourself now and take action.

Empower Your Now

Earlier in this chapter, we chatted about the illusion of time and the mirage that is the "perfect timing." Jumping back over to the JellyBeans video, we all know that our time is finite, limited, ever slipping through the hourglass that is life.

Thank you, Edgar Allen Poe, for the yet again morbid illustration of what life is.

You're more than welcome. Glad to have helped.

But all kidding aside, the question then is how do you step away from the illusion of the "perfect timing" and step towards your dreams?

You do that by Embracing The Power of Now.

There is no better time for you to begin to take action in the direction of your dreams than today, right here, right now.

It's a powerful thing when you start to approach your dreams from the position of "I'm gonna work on them today." "I'm gonna work on them right now."

Slowly and steadily, you begin to see your dreams take form. You begin to create a momentum that you are fueling continuously, and that is unstoppable. You start to feel the confidence of the fact that you can turn your dreams into reality and that you will. And then you look up, and you realize that you have accomplished everything that was on your heart, and you start asking, "what's next?"

One of the easiest and definitely extremely practical ways that I have found of embracing your now and going after your dreams today is the principle of the 5 Second Rule.

No, I'm not talking about the length of time that your Jolly Rancher can hit the floor and get put back in your mouth before it's classified as disgusting.... that's just science.

Hello McFly?!?

I am talking about the Mel Robbins principle of the 5 Second Rule.

If you have not read her book or watched her TEDx talk, I would highly recommend both, but here is the gist of the principle.

Mel found herself depressed, broke, losing it all, and not wanting to get out of bed. Her husband was losing the business. Her marriage was strained, and her bedroom covers had more appeal to them than the production of her day.

And I don't know about you... but I have been there! #Preach #Yas #NoMoreHashtags

Anyways. Mel was up late, flipping through the channels when she came across the countdown of a rocket ship just before takeoff, and a light bulb went off, and an epiphany happened.

That night as Mel lay in bed, she made the decision that in the morning, when that alarm clock went off, she wasn't just going to roll over, hit the snooze button, and go back to bed.

No! She was going to imagine she was that rocket ship, and she was going to countdown from 5.

5... 4... 3... 2... 1... Blast Off!

And the moment she was done counting down, she made the decision that she would launch herself out of bed.

And guess what?

The next morning when her alarm clock went off, it worked. For the first time in a long while, she jumped out of bed. Hit the ground. Turned off the snooze button and got about her day.

And then...

It worked the next day and the day after that.

And then Mel started to apply the 5 Second Rule to other areas of her life. Before she knew it, she wasn't just getting out of bed on time, but she was starting to have a massive breakthrough in all areas of her life.

But that wasn't the gamechanger.

The gamechanger was when she started sharing her success and the 5 Second Rule, and others like her started seeing the same success.

Why?

Because in that small action of counting down from 5, they all were embracing their fears, eliminating their distractions, and were empowering their now.

So, the next time you are thinking about your dreams, make the decision that you're going to count down from 5, and the moment you hit 1, blast off into the direction of taking action.

Let's give it a go and see what happens.

I promise you.

You won't regret it.

And if that doesn't get you off your ass, which it should, because you're a FREAKING Dreamcatcher, ask yourself this:

"If I had 30 seconds left to live, how would I be remembered?"

Cause at the end of the day, today is all we got. So, make today count.

12

Michelangelo Was Just Another Turtle Without Leonardo, Raphael, & Donatello. Facts!

I am a total Teenage Mutant Ninja Turtles fan. I mean fan with a capital F. I grew up when Ninja Turtles could and would only come on every Saturday. We had a strict rule in my house that Saturday cartoons weren't watched until <u>major chores</u> were done. So, I'd wake up before the sun, pledge the furniture, vacuum, clean the living room, take out the trash, and a lot more.

Look. You and I do not have enough time to go into the list that was "major chores." We would be here all day. Let's just say it was a LONG list that my mother required to be done before fun could be had.

Anyways. I would do all that before the house woke up so that I could watch my Ninja Turtles with a bowl of Cocoa Krispies on a Saturday like all good kids should.

But that's not where the fanboying stopped.

If you wanted to light my world up and make me the happiest kid on the block, you knew EXACTLY what to get me for my birthday, or for Christmas, or really for any other holiday.

My Aunt Mary Dee used to spoil me rotten. I would always look out for her mailed boxes or any time she came to visit because as much as I loved her, I also knew that with her came a fresh, straight out of the box, brand spanking new Teenage Mutant Ninja Turtle action figure.

My addiction to TMNT action figures *(those are the abbreviations for Teenage Mutant Ninja Turtles, for anyone who didn't know)* was so bad that not only was that the only gift I wanted as a present, and not only was that the show that I watched on Saturdays, but I also had a massive 90s, punch bowl-sized, Tupperware bowl for all my action figures.

Any time bath time was declared. Out came the bowl. I'd spend hours in the tub. The stories that I would create. The battles that would be had in that bathtub. The wars that would be fought by Shredder and the Teenage Mutant Ninja Turtles.

Some of my best memories growing up.

I remember there was a specific battle that I was acting out where I may or may not have attached an action figure to a living room lamp and then forgot about it, only to later discover that when the lights came on, that certain action figure melted under the heat. I loved my Teenage Mutant Ninja Turtles so much that I didn't care if my action figure's face was half-melted off. I still played with him.

He was now a 'zombie' mutant ninja turtle.

Hey, it made for an amazing backstory.

Now besides showing you how much of a TMNT nerd I was, the truth is, and I'll admit this, Michelangelo was just another turtle without his boy band clan of Leonardo, Raphael, Donatello, April, Splinter, and the infamous Casey Jones.

I mean, that's just facts! And you can't argue with facts.

Michelangelo wouldn't even be a Ninja Turtle if his sensei, Splinter, hadn't rescued all the turtles from accidentally getting dropped down a storm drain in New York.

Without his Teenage Mutant Ninja Turtles crew, Michelangelo would be living out of his mom's basement. Grubhubing pizza. Playing Fortnite. Fat. Lazy. Not even able to get off the couch.

But all kidding aside, though, we've all heard it said before, "your network is your net worth," or "show me your five friends, and I'll show you your future."

The problem is, what do you do when your network and your five friends don't match with where you want to go?

You know, that's one of the things that I struggled with for the absolute longest time. As a dreamer, I constantly was envisioning new things, and yet the people that I was with and the people that I was around didn't have that same drive or ambition to go after some of the bigger, better, and greater things in life.

So, I constantly wrestled back and forth with this notion of where do I find other Dreamcatchers?

Where do I find people that are like me, that want more in life, that want to be surrounded by greatness, that want to achieve the highest level possible, that want to accomplish everything that's on their heart?

Where do I find them?

As a Dreamcatcher, you are going to have to understand that your network breaks down into three crucial categories:

1. **Who are you learning from?**
   Or who are your mentors?

2. **Who is running alongside you?**
   Or who are your peers?

3. **And who are you teaching?**
   Or who are your followers?

Each one of those categories will define your network.

For a season, for me, I found people that were similar to me through going to live events. The only problem with going to events is that you meet them over the course of a weekend, and then they drop off the face of the planet afterward.

So, here's what I would recommend, and these are the things that I actually did, and that drastically changed my own life:

1. First thing is to be willing to <u>pay for proximity.</u>

<u>Be willing to pay for knowledge.</u>

I can't express to you how important this is. If you are seeking out mentors, you have to be willing to pay them for their time and for their knowledge. I know that some of the dilemmas that you're going to run into are, "well, I can't afford it."

Well, you can't <u>not</u> afford it.

You have to figure out a way to make it happen. If you can't afford the mentorships that they're offering, then get into their books, listen to their podcasts, follow their social media, reach out to them, and see if there's something that you can do to bring value to them and that will get you closer in proximity to them.

I'll be totally honest with you.

I could not find my mentors, and when I originally was seeking mentorship, I was dead broke. But I didn't allow that to stop me. I sought my mentors through any avenue that they were willing to give. I discovered avenues that allowed me to acquire my mentors for free, and I discovered avenues that my mentors were willing to give, but at the price point that I was able to pay.

So, what did that look like for me?

Well, I surrounded myself with my mentors and got into their mentorships they offered, way before I started paying them for it, and I did that by jumping into the following avenues:

- The books they wrote
- The YouTube channels they had and had posted
- The podcasts they launched
- The social media streams that they hosted and released

I even spent my time selling their products and their resources to their potential clients, all so that I could get one step closer to learning from them.

Then slowly, as I was able to build up capital, I then paid my mentors for their knowledge at the level that I could afford.

If you want to capture your dreams, if you want to turn your dream into reality, if you truly want to catch every one of your heart's desires, you have to be willing to learn from those that have been where you're at and have gone where you want to go.

Because although you could learn it all on your own, why would you?

If you had the ability to have somebody that could truly help you navigate the bumps, the obstacles, the hurdles that will come as you are going after your dream, then why would you not do whatever you could to learn from them?

Now a word of <u>caution</u> as you are looking for your mentors.

When you are picking a mentor, it's highly important to understand that there are a lot of 'posers' in our world. They flaunt a status that they are not really at, and they don't have the knowledge that they truthfully say they do.

So just like you would verify any investment you would ever make, when you were looking into mentorship and when you were looking who's voice you're going to listen to, and who's voice you're going to allow the time and attention inside of your head, you need to investigate that investment.

Because...

Your time is an investment.

Listening to their guidance is an investment.

Doing what they tell you to do is an investment.

If you bring in the wrong mentor, the wrong voice, then guess what, I'm going to tell you, you're going to go off course and not go where you should've gone, to begin with.

So don't look up to the "wannabe" gurus, the "posers," the ones that just flash. Those are the ones you want to stay away from.

Really look for the ones that have put in the long hours, the time, the detail, who have the results, and have lasted and the ups and the downs.

Get in proximity of those mentors.

2. The second thing is to be willing to investigate who's around you

Who are you surrounding yourself with?

Who is in your peer group?

Who are the Dreamcatchers that you are with, that are going after things, that are challenging themselves, that are having ups and downs, that can support you when you're going through your ups and downs, and that you can support when they're going through their ups and downs?

And if the answer is you are not around those types of people, then my follow-up question to you is, where do you go to find other Dreamcatchers?

Well, you have to get resourceful. You have to get creative. You have to be willing to think outside the norm.

Because other Dreamcatchers are out there. I promise you that. They are all around you. They are looking for you as much as you are looking for them. You just have to know where to look.

One of the ways that I chose to find other Dreamcatchers was I started and hosted a podcast called The Dreamcatcher Show. I ran it for two seasons, was able to get it to an Apple top-rated show, and I was able to connect with some amazing people.

But if I were just going to be completely honest with you, one of the main reasons that I started that podcast was so that I could link arms with other Dreamcatchers, learn from other Dreamcatchers, hear their Dreamcatcher stories, be inspired by them, develop a relationship with them, network with them, and at the end of the day, bring value their way as well as bring value my way.

Now, I'm not saying that everybody has to go out and start a podcast in order to bring in the peer group that you're looking for.

But I will tell you, it worked, and I am so glad I did.

One of the other things that I did to investigate those around me that I would <u>HIGHLY</u> recommend you do as well is I cleaned up my social media platforms.

I will caution you though, this hurt some people's feelings, and I definitely got some backlash for it, but I literally went through each one of my social media accounts and cleared them out.

What do I mean?

Well, I literally went through everybody and anybody that was not bringing value to me, that was not where I was *(someone who was going after their own dreams and trying to accomplish more in their life,)* or that wasn't at a whole nother level from where I was *(somebody that I could look up to, learn from, and inspired to be.)*

And I cut them out of my social media entirely. Unfollowed them. Unliked their posts. Unlistened to their social media presence.

Why?

Because it used to be that your peer group was just the watering hole that you hung out at.

It was just the water tank at the office.

It was just the pub that you got drinks at.

The issue is our peer groups can no longer be contained to just that. Your peer group is no longer just the people that you are in proximity with, who you can 'rub shoulders with.' It is much larger than that. Our world has grown and stretched. It's so easy for you and

211

me to connect with somebody across the world and for them to be able to connect right back.

Your social media has to be something that you do not neglect. It is one of the avenues that is an example of your five friends.

So, you've got to clean it up, and here's the parameters that I would recommend for that clean-up. Ask yourself:

> Does it inspire you?
> Does it challenge you?
> Does it help you?
> Will it take you to your dreams and your goals?

If your answer back is "no," then clean them up and cut them out.

Also, little <u>EXTRA</u> credit for those that want to go above and beyond.

You want to really make a difference in your Dreamcatcher world?

Take those same parameters above and evaluate the movies you watch, the shows you stream, the podcasts you listen to, the books you read.

Take those same parameters and evaluate all areas of your Dreamcatcher life.

3. And lastly, ask yourself, "<u>who are you teaching?</u>"

No, I am not saying you need to go and write a book.

No, I am not saying you need to start posting motivational social media posts on the regular.

No, I am not saying you need to start a YouTube channel, launch a course, release a podcast, stand on a soapbox, and preach.

But what I am saying is...

Who are you teaching?

Who are you helping?

Who are you inspiring?

Who are you leading?

One of the best ways for you to learn anything is to teach it back. If you truly are going to learn how to be a Dreamcatcher, then the way to learn the artform is to bring someone alongside you and help them become a Dreamcatcher too.

Heck, if all you do is hand this book to another potential Dreamcatcher, then you are teaching someone else exactly what you, yourself, have learned.

213

The Art of Dreamcatching

13

You Wanna Know the Thing I DESPISE As A Dreamcatcher?!?!

It's having to be patient and wait on my dreams to manifest themselves.

Like I get it, you have to put in the work.
You have to get stronger.
You have to learn the lessons that need to be learned.
But why does it have to take so LLLLOOOOONNNGGGG?

If there has been any major pitfall to my life, a constant thorn in my side, a pain in my ass, it has been not giving my dreams the time necessary for them to show up.

I don't know if you are anything like me, but mentally, I 'understand' the concept.

I understand that, especially with new skills or large goals, that time is necessary. It's a given. It has to happen. I know that it takes hundreds upon hundreds of years for the Redwood trees to become the Redwood trees.

I GET IT!!!!!

But the problem is that even with that understanding, I put myself on a timeline. Sure, before I start going after the dream, I think it's a very generous timeframe, but more times than not, it's not. And more times than not, it's nowhere even close to the right time frame.

This is generally what happens... Let me play it out for you, play by play.

I get all excited.

I am going to make this happen.

Isn't it going to be awesome when it does happen?

Oh, I can't wait.

Let me see... how long should it take?

Let's take that time and double it. Heck, let's triple it.

Then I start working on the dream.

Wait, it's not happening to the tune that I thought it was going to.

Then I start to stress out.

I start to get irritated with my dreams and the fact that they are not appearing.

And if I am not careful, I end up throwing that dream to the wind all because I wasn't patient with it.

Sound familiar?

Let me be completely frank with you. If you want to be a Dreamcatcher, you have to learn the art of patience. It is a skill set that is required. Nothing worthy of talking about hasn't had to put in the time necessary for it to appear.

Listen.

If I could wave a magic wand and remove the unnecessary element of patience, you best believe it would have already been waved.

The sad thing is that as I look back at my life, I gave up a lot of great opportunities simply because I wasn't patient with them. And, the really, really sad thing about those opportunities, in a lot of those situations, I was naturally talented. But I threw them to the wind because they were just taking way too long.

Perfect example.

I have always been rhythmically gifted. Not like dance rhyme. More like, I was able to keep a beat, and as a kid, I loved the drums.

And so, I begged my parents over and over again for them to allow me to learn to play. I asked for the drum set. I begged for the lessons. I knew I was meant to be a drummer. My parents eventually caved in and got me the drum set and set me up with the lessons.

I can still remember the day I sat behind the symbols and realized that this was it. I was now officially a drummer. I grabbed the wooden sticks and set to learning the instrument.

At first, the natural talent came to the top. I could carry a decent beat, but once the lessons started, it all went downhill.

Why?

Because I was a naturally born drummer.

"Why couldn't I figure out how to carry a beat and use the kick pedal at the same time?"

I mean, I could focus on the snare. I could carry the beat with the kick pedal separately. But when you asked me to put them together, I was a lost cause.

´ And what happened? I got extremely frustrated with myself.

"This should be easy," I thought. "Why was I having such a hard time learning this?"

"How come I couldn't get this right away?"

"Why was this so difficult for me?"

And then the inevitable happened. The very thing that I was so excited for suddenly became the very thing I despised and hated. I suddenly lost interest and did not want to be a drummer any longer.

Looking back, it's really quite simple to understand what happened. I wasn't patient with myself or the drums and therefore gave up on something that truthfully could have been amazing.

How many times have you found you have done that very same thing in your life?

Maybe with the new job?

Or the new business?

Or the weight loss challenge?

Or the college degree you were so excited for?

Or the new relationship you were so pumped to get into?

What happened? Are you sure that it "just wasn't right" for you? Or if we were truthful with each other, did you put unrealistic expectations on the situation, on yourself, on the other person, and not give it enough time to come to be?

My mentors put it this way, and I love this.

Stop putting a time limit on your dreams.

When you do this, you are already DOOMING your dreams to failure.

How about, instead of saying, it HAS to happen at this date, or before this time, or it has to go this certain way, why don't you change that mindset?

Why don't you start to say, "I will persist until I see success." "I will continue until it happens."

I mean, seriously, isn't that releasing to think about?
Doesn't that just take some weight off your shoulders?

Now, I want to clarify for everyone real quick.

Patience is not saying, "Someday, I'll start the project." Patience is putting in the work and effort every single day until a breakthrough happens. Patience is pushing and working and learning and growing and getting better and going after the goal even when you do not see any results, even when it appears that you are going backwards rather than forwards.

Oh… and you really want to get me hot under the collar?!?

Have me put in the time and effort and then have me go BACKWARDS?

Are you joking me?

Like why did I even start if I am going to go BACKWARDS?

But it's all part of being a Dreamcatcher.

Here's the beautiful thing. Take my dream. My dream to be an international New York Times bestselling author. My books are sought after, and they are read across the globe. I inspire. I motivate. I influence. I help others take action and catch their dreams through my writings.

That's my dream. That is me as a Dreamcatcher. But think about this. I can accomplish that dream when I am thirty-five. I can accomplish that dream when I am hundred and thirty-five.

I still have accomplished the dream, and I am still a Dreamcatcher, either way.

So, when I release myself of the pressure of it "HAS TO HAPPEN NOW" or by this date, and instead I focus on the tasks necessary to make it happen, the beautiful thing is, it eventually will happen.

It's all just a matter of time and me being patient.

It's like "the engine that could."

He eventually gets up the hill. He just had to keep going.

When I released my first book, "*The Pen and Its Author*," I knew I had a problem with expectations and being patient, and I tried to prepare myself.

My goal: To get my first book to be an Amazon bestseller.

Well, on launch date, it didn't look like that was going to happen. I had put in all the work. Had written the book. Gotten it self-published. Found the editor. Researched the right categories. Reached out to my network before the launch date. Submitted the book to all the book promo sites. I did everything I should have in order to accomplish my goal.

But on the launch date, it didn't look like it was going to happen. It looked like the book was going to be a flop, and I had to have a real conversation with myself.

"Is this going to be the end? Are we going to give up because our first attempt didn't have the success we wanted it to have? Are we going to throw in the towel simply because the first time we published, it didn't become the bestseller that we wanted it to become?"

Then I had to ask the tough question,

"What is my ultimate goal?"

"International New York Times Bestselling Author."

That's the goal. That's the dream.

"So, if it's our first book that gets us there, GREAT. If it's our fifth, fantastic. If it's our hundredth, AMAZING."

"Well then, are we going to stop writing because our first book didn't have the success we were hoping for?

223

Or are we going to continue writing until we get to see our name next to the title International New York Times Bestselling Author?"

That's the same sort of conversation that you have to have with yourself and with your dreams. Your dreams are too important for you not to have that conversation.

Don't be like me and my failed drum lesson.

Make the choice now that it doesn't matter how long it takes, you are going to accomplish your dreams NO MATTER what happens.

Oh, and on a side note, "The Pen and Its Author" did eventually become an Amazon bestseller in five different categories.

I just didn't give it enough time to do so.

A little lesson on patience

The Art of Dreamcatching

14

It's The Final Countdown... But Only When You Say It Is

My hands gripped the wall.

My focus lasered in. I had never felt this sheer amount of fear before. Oh, I had been in this spot before, but never under the same conditions.

These conditions were completely brand new to me.

This was the moment that I was going to die.

Taking one hand off the wall, I held firm to where I was at. I had to allow myself to rest. That was why I was here, to begin with. I hadn't allowed myself to rest.

Stupid!

This was very much both my fault and something that only a rookie would have made the mistake of.

I looked around for my options.

"No. I can't go there." I thought to myself.

Taking a moment to adjust and look for another answer.

"No. I can't go there."

I needed to hurry. I could feel fatigue setting in, and I had to make a decision quickly before it did.

I hugged the wall even more as I looked for answers. *"My foot won't go there."*

"What do I do?" I asked myself.

"How stupid could I have been?"

"Why didn't I wait?"

"Why did I try to rush it?"

"Look where we are at now?"

"Snap out of it, John. None of those questions will help you where you are now. We have to come up with a solution. We have to, or this is the day that we die."

The inner dialogue racing through my head. I had to find a way to get out of this situation. I knew that. I knew I was in grave, mortal danger if I could not figure out how to resolve this.

I looked back.

That was what I was trying to avoid.

I could not do that, or it meant death for sure.

I quickly assessed my options.

I had nowhere to go. Nowhere.

And so, I jumped. I pushed off and jumped.

Let me give you a little backstory to this time and space before I give you the resolve.

It was my first real attempt at being an entrepreneur. I had always looked up to them. The freedoms they had. The ability to make choices that others couldn't. The way they viewed the world and the changes they brought about because of their ventures.

Man. I wanted to be one, and as a Dreamcatcher, you better believe I had all the ideas.

All of them.

But this was my first real attempt at acting on one of my dreams.

This was it. I knew it. This was my moment. This was going to be what made me. I was going to join the ranks of the entrepreneurs that I had always looked up to.

My dream.

It was going to take me there.

My dream.

It was going to revolutionize the industry.

I still find myself walking down the aisles of a grocery store and seeing the now 'overcrowded space' that my dream would have been a part of. I still walk down those aisles and realize that although there are many 'knock-offs' of my dream, mine was entirely different from all the competitors that are now in the space.

What was my dream?

Oh, the idea was brilliant.

The concept was there.

I had spent a year developing just the concept.

A year of putting in all the work for the idea.

It was groundbreaking.

It was revolutionary.

It was my baby, and to this day, I still have not seen anything like it.

This was going to be "it." This was going to be what set me on the course of my dreams.

I was going to bring to the market a revolutionary supplement company that would alter the way performance supplements were consumed.

I had created the perfect supplement formula. It was groundbreaking, and the best part was that the formula actually worked. It wasn't hype.

It worked!

I had worked back and forth with the manufacturing company to get my product just right. I had tested the formula on several different types of athletes. I had perfected the packaging. I had sourced the right partnerships and created the brand that would launch this supplement company. Everything seemed to be lining up.

There was one, one minor problem.

Small, but I had figured out how to take care of that problem.

The problem?

The problem was although I had created the 'perfect' product, my partner and I had no way of funding the production of our product.

So… maybe it was a little bit bigger of a problem than what I had alluded to.

But I had it all figured out. I knew exactly what we were going to do. I knew the answer, and everything was working out.

At the time, crowdsourcing had only just started to create momentum, and I knew this was our avenue for funding my baby. I studied over and over again different successful crowdsourcing campaigns and knew exactly how we were going to launch our crowdsourcing campaign.

Our product spoke to all different types of athletes. The skaters. The surfers. The bodybuilders. The rock climbers. If you were in a sport and you wanted to have optimal performance, this was the product that would help you see your peak.

So, I decided that our crowdsourcing video would showcase all different types of athletes, all performing at the highest level.

It was amazing.

We filmed skaters and surfers. We got footage of bodybuilders doing extreme workouts. We filmed traceurs parkouring over all different types of obstacles. We took the time getting the best angles and shots of our extreme athletes doing what they did best.

It was all coming together. The footage looked amazing. I knew that this was going to be a remarkable, successful crowdsourced campaign and that this was going to be what was going to get our funding.

The week prior. We had filmed our rock climbers, me included, in an extreme version of the sport called free climbing. These are the guys who traverse rock faces without ropes and climb their hearts out.

The problem was when we were filming our free climbers, it just wasn't right. The angles were off. The scenes were horrible, and it did not convey the extreme that I wanted our viewers and, eventually, our customers seeing, so I made the decision that we would film it the following week.

The day of our reshoot, our main free climber phones me up and lets me know that he is horribly sick and will not be able to climb. I'd have to climb alone.

That's okay. He and I had been climbing together for a while, so I made the decision I would just step in and take his place and get the filming done.

We were in a time crunch and needed to get our crowdsourcing video up and loaded so that we could launch our campaign.

Now.

Before I can go any further, here is what I need you to understand about free climbing. It is a calculated sport. Free climbers map out the rocks that they are climbing so that they know where to go when they are on the rock face. As a free climber, you practice inside rock climbing gyms under mats so that you can build the strength necessary to climb out amongst mother nature.

And one last thing about a free climber, one that is extremely important about climbing, a free climber must rest.

They need to take breaks between climbs. This allows their muscles to relax. Their forearm strength to return and ultimately allows them to climb again.

Well, on the day…

I did not have another climber to climb with. We needed to get this part of the day filmed so that we could move onto the next setup and start filming there.

The morning started out great.

The rock face that I was climbing was larger than the one we had climbed before. Roughly a total of 30 feet, but I had mapped it out. I knew the direction that I was going to take in order to get to the top.

The first climb went amazing. Made it to the top with no issues, but the footage was not doing the 30-foot face justice.

"Let's do it again," I told the film crew.

And so, we did it again a second time.

And then we did it again a third time.

When I came down the rock face to look at the footage after the third retake, it just wasn't conveying the masterpiece of the climb. Stepping away from the camera, I walked with the filmographer and showed him the angles I was looking for.

"Here's what I want you to do. As I am climbing up the mountain, I want you to start at the base of the climb. Then I want you to follow me up the face as I climb. Slowly, as you are following me up, I want you to get closer to the mountain so that by the end of the footage, you are looking up the entire thing with me at the top."

This next bit would be easy.

All we had to do was get the footage, and then we were out of there. I had already climbed this three other times. The fourth was going to be a cakewalk.

The problem.

I had not been resting. I had been jumping right back up and climbing right after I had already finished climbing it already.

But I did not know this was the problem. I felt great. My energy felt fantastic. Everything seemed perfect.

I only realized we were in trouble when I moved my foot into a spider position 20 feet up in the air and realized I didn't know where to go next. I was stuck, and to make matters worse, my forearm strength was now fading and fading fast.

Oh, and one other problem

At the bottom of the face that I was free climbing were these massive, jagged, sharp rocks that jutted out from the ground. No problem if you are walking over them. Big problem if you are now suspended in the air 20 feet with no sense of direction, no sense of how to get up the mountain, or how to get down.

And so there I was.

Snugged against a rock.

Holding on for dear life to a root that was jutting out from the rock face.

Hanging there with these two choices to make:

1. Do I hold on for as long as I can, eventually lose my strength, and fall back and land on the jagged rocks? If I do that, I run the risk of breaking my back, having severe head damage, and having a high chance of dying.

Or

2. Do I push off of this face, pray for the best, and hope to clear the rocks that are below?

And that is what I did.

I went with option number two. I'd like to say that I landed in a bed of roses, with pillows all around me, and floated down on clouds as a way of comfort, but that's not what happened.

Instead, I landed on a cement sidewalk, in a *(and I'm proud of this)* perfect squat, but a squat doesn't do anything for the body, correct form or not, when you are jumping from 20 feet and landing on concrete cement. I immediately shattered my heel and my ankle upon impact. Once that support was gone, I fell on my side and, without knowing it, shattered my elbow and broke my wrist.

I was in so much pain that on the way to the hospital, the medics had to jab me three times with morphine, and the pain still did not subside.

All of that, though, was not even the worst part.

The worst part did not come until 3am. I lay there on the couch. With my entire right side broken, unable to get comfortable, the pain medication wearing off, staring up at the ceiling, the realization came to me. I was a failure.

<u>My dream had failed.</u>

"How could a father of two (at the time) and the sole provider for my family be SO STUPID?

What was I thinking?

How in the world did I think that "me," John Bourgeois, could join the ranks of the entrepreneurs that

I looked up to? How did I expect to build a revolutionary company and change the world?

What was I thinking?

Do you see what dreaming does?" I asked myself.

"It breaks you.

Dreaming is for someone else. I am not worthy of dreaming and catching my dreams.

Why did I even try?

Now I was going to have to be out of work for at least 6 months or longer. I was confined to a couch, not able to take showers, not able to drive. My doctor told me I would never be able to be 'as physically active again' and that I would 'probably never run again."

My dream had not just failed.
<u>My dream had failed me.</u>

"This is what they warn you about." I thought to myself.

"Why couldn't I just be satisfied with what I had?

Why did I always have to be looking for more?

Why did I always have to be dreaming and envisioning a better way of life for myself?

Why couldn't I just settle?

Why couldn't I just be like everyone else?

Why did I have to be different?

What was I thinking?"

And in that moment, for whatever reason, I pulled out my cell phone, and I opened up Facebook. I don't know why I was on. I probably was just trying to numb the pain, and as I was scrolling, I came across this post:

Kobe Bryant
April 13, 2013

"This is such BS! All the training and sacrifice just flew out the window with one step that I've done millions of times! The frustration is unbearable. The anger is rage. Why the hell did this happen?!? Makes no damn sense. Now I'm supposed to come back from this and be the same player Or better at 35?!? How in the world am I supposed to do that??

I have NO CLUE. Do I have the consistent will to overcome this thing? Maybe I should break out the rocking chair and reminisce on the career that was.

Maybe this is how my book ends.

Maybe Father Time has defeated me…

Then again, maybe not! It's 3:30am, my foot feels like dead weight, my head is spinning from the pain meds and I'm wide awake. Forgive my Venting but what's the purpose of social media if I won't bring it to you Real No Image??

Feels good to vent, let it out. To feel as if THIS is the WORST thing EVER!

Because After ALL the venting, a real perspective sets in.

There are far greater issues/challenges in the world then a torn Achilles.

Stop feeling sorry for yourself, find the silver lining and get to work with the same belief, same drive and same conviction as ever.

One day, the beginning of a new career journey will commence. Today is NOT that day.

"If you see me in a fight with a bear, prey for the bear"*. Ive always loved that quote. Thats "mamba mentality" we don't quit, we don't cower, we don't run. We endure and conquer.*

I know it's a long post but I'm Facebook Venting LOL. Maybe now I can actually get some sleep and be excited for surgery tomorrow.

First step of a new challenge.

Guess I will be Coach Vino the rest of this season. I have faith in my teammates. They will come thru.

Thank you for all your prayers and support. Much Love Always.

Mamba Out."

This is the final chapter of The Art of Dreamcatching, but it is not your final chapter unless you decide that it is. Now is your turn to rise up and take charge.

Yes. There will be hurdles.

Yes. You will have to start, stop, pivot, adjust, change, evolve, grow, expand, but you, as a Dreamcatcher, get to decide when the book is finished.

You get to decide when the last chapter is written and when your story is finally done. Do not allow anyone else to tell you differently. Tune out the noise. Stop listening to the critic. See yourself for who you really are and go out there and catch you some dreams.

<u>Dreamcatcher, I wrote this book for you</u>. I wrote it with you in mind. I wrote it so that you can go and turn ANY dream into a reality.

Take what you have learned here and apply it to your world and to your life.

You are a Dreamcatcher.

And now is your time.

I'll see you on the other side.

And I cannot wait to hear all that you have accomplished!

Go get them, Dreamcatcher.

Turn that Dream of yours into reality

Resources

For those of you that are interested in diving further into becoming more of your Dreamcatcher self, I am going to provide for you some of the resources that have helped me on my own journey of catching my dreams. Hopefully you'll find the same value in it that I did for myself. Note: the resources below are ones that I've revisited every year and found additional pieces of value in them as I do. Enjoy!

Books:

You Are a Badass: How to Stop Doubting Your Greatness and Start Living an Awesome Life *by Jen Sincero*

Hands down this book has changed my life. I am now on my second copy of this book because I continue to find new value in it every time I read it. I came across this book when I was going through my messy divorce, and I am so glad that I did.

This book helped me discover who I was and what I was and reminded me of the 'Badass' that I am without anyone else's approval of it.

Highly recommend this book!

240

The Alchemist *by Paulo Coelho*

Oh my goodness! Another MUST read! This is less in the 'self help' section of the bookstore and more in the 'fiction' section, but it is still a vital read. You are not going to have exercises or 'how to(s)' in this book. It is written in a parable/fable fashion, but man, does it hit home.

The entire book is based on a shepherd boy going after his dreams and the journey along the way to catching them.

If you don't trust my recommendation, then maybe trust Will Smith's and Oprah's :)

Millionaire Success Habits: The Gateway To Wealth & Prosperity *by Dean Graziosi*

You want some practical exercises to level up your Dreamcatcher skillset, then this is definitely a book that you should read.

In fact one of the exercises in this book comes directly from Dean Graziosi.

I recommend that you have a pen and piece of paper with you and that you stop along the way to execute the exercises within the book.

Dean has done a great job of simplifying the skills and steps needed for success, so my recommendation, do the work and you'll get the results.

Jump: Take The Leap of Faith To Achieve Your Life of Abundance *by Steve Harvey*

This was the book that I was reading around the time that my grandfather passed away. Talk about the right place at the right time.

The entire book talks about the importance of stepping into your dreams now versus pushing them off to a later date, and Steve shares from his own story, incidents where he jumped, and incidents where he didn't but wished he did.

Added bonus, Steve does a great job of adding in bits of humor along the way. I found myself laughing out loud at different points as I read.

The Magic of Thinking Big: Acquire The Secrets of Success... Achieve Everything You've Always Wanted *by David J. Schwartz, Ph.D.*

Newer to my collection, but I tell you, it will be circling in my reread section every year from here on out.

Why? Because it's a great book in reminding you of the importance and the power of thinking big.

One of the problems that we can have as Dreamcatchers, especially when you are first starting out, is you can allow yourself to dream too small. It's a fear mechanism. We do not want to miss the target therefore we make the target very easy to hit.

But this book is a great reminder for why you should continue to aim for the stars and shares with you real life examples of others who aimed for their BIG dreams and caught them.

Act Like A Success Think Like A Success: Discover Your Gift And The Way To Life's Riches *by Steve Harvey*

One of the challenges with being a Dreamcatcher is making sure that your mindset is where it needs to be when it needs to be there. It's the whole concept of 'rinsing out your glass.'

And Steve breaks it down for you in his book both how to think like a success, the importance of it, and what it will do for you and your life when you make the decision to.

This book is an easy read and something that you can immediately start to apply to your own Dreamcatcher.